New Orleans

Ghosts III

Victor C. Klein

ISBN 0-9661812-5-5

Library of Congress Catalog Card Number pending

Design Production: Victor C. Klein

Published by Lycanthrope Press
PO Box 9028
Metairie, LA 70005-9028
L. Talbot, Senior Editor
(504) 866-9756
www.ordotempliveritatis.org

Dedication

*To my mother Juliette Couret Klein
who has and will love me into eternity.*

and

Jeannie Faye Jasim — my Salvation.

Table of Contents

Introduction

A revolution began in the 1990's of which *New Orleans Ghosts* played a significant role locally (New Orleans) and a minor but notable role nationally. That revolution in popular culture was a national renewal in paranormal phenomena generally, and a specific interest in ghosts, hauntings, specters, revenants which have invaded the media over the past decade.

To prove my point consider these three facts. Before I wrote *New Orleans Ghosts*, there existed only one locally generated book about our restless, dear departed *Ghost Stories of Old New Orleans*, authored by Jeanne deLavigne (1946). Since the publication of <u>New Orleans Ghosts</u> (1993), almost a dozen works on the genre have found their way to the retail shelves (see my bibliography).

Virtually every night in the U.S.A. one can surface a television program about haunted cities, hotels, battlefields, etc. Personally, I have appeared on the Travel Channel, Arts and Entertainment, History Channel, National Geographic Special, etc., etc. Whenever a T.V. production company comes to New Orleans to document our ghosts they inevitably call on me.

My works have single-handedly changed the thrust of the tourism industry in the French Quarter. Ghost tours far outnumber any other type in the area. Even those which do not specialize in *spectres* inevitably mention some ghostly occurrence excised from my works.

When I published *New Orleans Ghosts II* (2000), I described the methodology I followed in researching both works. I used deLavigne's classic tome as base point, but enriched it by seeking other sources. These other sources were newspaper stories and books about ghosts generally which contained sometimes one, sometimes several stories about the ectoplasmic entities of our fair city.

I also included addresses, bibliographic references, footnotes, indexes, maps, appendices and actual photographs in order to give my efforts a degree of scientific respectability. The formula obviously worked.

New Orleans Ghosts III represents my continuing interest and research into the realm of the dead. The format continues in this effort with one exception. Many of the books that have been generated by my originals contain stories of which I was unaware through my initial methodology. I include them in this recent work and provide the proper citations.

The salient reason I continue the episodes is to encourage others to contemplate and explore that greatest of all mysteries–Death!   My success in this effort has been overwhelming, considering the media interest and research generated by what I have done so far.

If life after death could ever be proved through consistently demonstrable criteria, then our concepts and delusions concerning our humanity would be forever transformed. The western death denials systems that we call religions would be exposed and revealed as what they are in actuality — internal constructs whose only substance is the terror of death.

House Guests II

In *New Orleans Ghosts II,* I included a chapter that listed the names, addresses, phone numbers, and average price per double occupancy of thirteen hotels that are alleged to be haunted. The hotels were listed alphabetically. This chapter was a great idea. It provided tourists and locals with documented hauntings so they could hopefully have a private, intimate encounter with the restless spirits of the dead.

I limited the chapter to thirteen stories intending to include another thirteen documented haunted hotels for *New Orleans Ghosts III.* Here they are. The same format is followed here as was articulated in *New Orleans Ghost II.* All hotels are listed alphabetically and include addresses, phone numbers, and the prices for double occupancy as of date of publication (2004). The area code for all hotels is "504". I use the traditional French designation "rue" (street) to indicate locales in the French Quarter. Ten of the stories were surfaced from *Journey into Darkness.. . Ghosts and Vampire,* and cited as Smith, Kalila Katherina with page number. The other three stories will be given proper bibliographic citations.

Ashley House of Avenue Plaza
($125; varies seasonally)
2111 St. Charles Avenue
529-2274

The history of this hotel is ripe for ghostly manifestations. Built in 1841 as a private residence, it has been the scene of a jealousy inspired murder, and the cruelties of slavery. During the Civil War, it served as an infirmary and a prison for Confederate soldiers. The horrors that transpired behind those walls can scarce be imagined.

Kalila Katherina Smith, an author and reputable ghost enthusiast, asserts, "We have concluded that it [the site] probably contains one of the highest concentrations of spirits of any building that we have investigated" (Smith, p. 88).

1891 Castle Inn Bed & Breakfast
($89- $159)
1539 Fourth Street
(The Garden District)

This is a very haunted hotel. It is located in the Garden District in uptown New Orleans in a beautiful stone mansion replete with suits of armor, antiques and theme rooms. There are numerous phenomena at play here. Objects disappear. Spheres of light blink on and off. Spirit voices abound. You really need to check this one out. It's fabulous! (Smith, p. 89-90.)

Crescent on Canal
(Rates vary seasonally)
1732 Canal Street
70112
524-7352

Something is amiss at this imposing hotel. Since it was erected in the mid-twentieth century, it has housed three different facilities: Claiborne Towers, Pallas Hotel, and now The

Crescent on Canal. After the failure of each enterprise, the building lay fallow for protracted periods of time. This is odd since the edifice occupies a prime location in the virtual heart of the city. During these periods of abandonment reports of lights in the deserted building stimulated a flood of police and fire inspections that apprehended no culprits or trespassers.

The alleged hauntings are varied. Strange occurrences transpire on the third elevator. Lights are seen on, as yet, unoccupied floors. A "misty, dancing apparition" has been witnessed in the main ballroom (Smith, p. 70).

Check in. Not only will you have a great view of New Orleans' downtown district, you may also experience a haunting.

Dauphine Orleans Hotel May Bailey's
($99 and up)
415 Dauphine Street
70112
586-1800

New Orleans was the scene of one of the most successful social experiments in history. From 1898 to 1917, prostitution was legal and confined to a section of town that came to be known as "Storyville." It is alleged that the spirits of passion haunt this site (Smith, p. 72).

Historic French Market Inn
($134; varies seasonally)
501 Rue Decatur
70130
561-5621

Here is a ghost story that has been seconded by a professional parapsychologist completely by chance. Carol Guess, a ghost hunter with Ghost Labs, visited New Orleans a few years ago. Having more than just a passing interest in things that go bump in the night, she decided to experience the

"Haunted History Ghost Tour." Upon arriving in New Orleans, she checked into Room 218. Around 10:00 P.M., she was literally bombarded by unexplainable events. She felt the "presence" of unseen male visitors; her unset alarm clock cried out again and again; the shower started and stopped in staccato sequences; she heard loud noises of uncertain origin. The most chilling experience was the manifestation of a bloody palm print on her bed sheet. As she examined this ghoulish artifact, it suddenly vanished.

On the tour, she related her experiences to her guide and the group. It is from this testimony that the story has been recorded and retold in my work (Smith, p. 72).

Hotel St. Pierre
($149; varies seasonally)
911 Burgundy
70116
524-4401

This hotel is actually a conglomeration of buildings moved from various sites in the Quarter. The majority of these were slave quarters. It is haunted by a somewhat friendly Confederate soldier and several other disembodied souls (Montz, pp. 118-119).

Pontchartrain Hotel
($89-259)
2031 St. Charles Avenue
70140
524–581

Built in 1927 with 119 rooms, a sophisticate piano bar, and a refined dining room, which features Creole and Cajun specialities, this hotel is among the finest in the city.

During the 1950's, it served as an exclusive residential hotel for some 35 permanent residents who called the Pontchartrain home during this period. The individuals were older, wealthy patrons who preferred the convenience of a hotel over a large home with its upkeep and security concerns. Mr. Douglas Leman, an employee of the hotel, related the story of two affluent, reclusive sisters who dwelled on the ninth floor. After these residents died their shades remained. They are peaceful ghosts who chat between themselves and roam the ninth floor. (Smith, p. 83.) Mr. Leman also related a story about a socially prominent gentleman he called "Mr. B." This man only appeared at night and never ate or drank — in public. Mr. Leman suspected he was a vampire!

Prince Conti Hotel - The Bombay Room (Bar)
($99; varies seasonally)
830 Conti Street
70112
529-4172

Sit down. Relax. Have an Absinthe Frappé or a Ramous Gin Fizz. After you've bolstered your coverage, move over to booth #3. If she's not busy tampering with the electrical equipment in the kitchen or roaming around the hotel, you might be joined by a revenant of a storyville madame who died in one of the hotel's cozy rooms (Smith, p. 106).

Prytania Inn
($49 - $59)
1507 Prytania Street
70130
566-1515

Not only am I a writer and paranormal investigator, but also a practicing occultist and ceremonial magician. As such, I have participated in many seances and magical rituals. These activities depend on a variety of factors. Among them are the proper environment and setting. Such elements are found in Room #9 where many Halloween parties and seances have been conducted with varying successes. Many years ago, a child by the name Isabel died a tragic death due to a fall. It is her shade that has allegedly created a perfect arena for experiencing the unknown.

Radisson Hotel
($129 - $209)
1500 Canal Street
70112
522-4500

This grand, elegant hotel has hosted many of the world's rich and famous. Its beautifully appointed design has furnished joy and pleasure to countless guests; however, it has also been the scene of several tragic deaths. One hapless chap fell to his death down an elevator shaft, and another individual committed suicide behind the "do not disturb" sign posted outside his room. Today, employees and guests report a silent, shadowy male figure dressed in a Bogart-era trench coat who vanishes in the elevator.

St. Vincent Guest House
($59-$99)
1507 Magazine Street
70130
523-3411

This place is steeped in tragic history. Built in 1861 by the Daughters of Charity it was dedicated to the care of orphans. In the days before abortion and birth control, orphans were a much greater burden than today.

During the Civil War, it was used by Union forces to detain Confederate prisoners. Many died. The twentieth century witnessed its use as a home for unwed mothers. Certainly, many tears flowed behind these red brick walls (Ibid, p. 84).

On 1 May 2003, I interviewed chambermaid Rhonda Chiles. She related innumerable stories about the ghostly laughter of children, moved furniture, and various spectral appearances.

Southern Nights Bed & Breakfast
(Rates vary)
1827 S. Carrollton Avenue
486-4211?

In the latter part of the eighteenth century, this splendid Greek revival mansion was the home of Pierre Cormier, his wife Cecelia, their child Katie, and Pierre's brother, Jean Phillip. The two brothers were reckless men who enjoyed drinking, gaming, carriage and horse races. As the city prepared for yet another late summer's hurricane, the brothers opted for a carriage race in the driven downpour which is a signature of these ponderous storms. The race ended in blood and death. Pierre's carriage lost traction on the slick, muddied road. It tumbled over killing Cecilia instantly and forever crippling hapless little Katie.

It is said that Cecelia's shade continued to keep vigil over the paralyzed girl until her death several years later. Even Katie's premature demise did not dampen Cecelia's vigil. Her ghost has been witnessed in Rooms 2 and 3, accompanied by the sweet smell of her gardenia perfume.

Ursulines Guest House
($60 - $70 average)
708 rue Ursulines, 70116
525-8509

I don't know if it's haunted, but it is inexpensive and located smack-dab in the middle of the Quarter.

The Muffled Bells

In a cramped, dark stifling French Quarter walk-up a man lay in a clammy stupor. Cheap street drugs, and even cheaper booze helped chase away the vandals who tore across the fractured windows of his mind. His eyes fluttered. Consciousness ebbed. The cigarette gripped by quivering fingers fell.

Smoke — then a smoldering fire that gave birth to great daemon like clouds of more smoke invaded the box-like cubicle our soon to be victim called "home". His eyes flickered open. The daemon smoke had occupied his lungs. He coughed, choked. The blemished nightmare of his desperate life was gone from his mind. His only thought was survival. He struggled to his feet keeping his head as close to the floor as possible. Still the daemon smoke hammered his lungs and slashed his eyes. Pain and fear replaced crack cocaine and liquor. Panic soon joined the party and our unlucky friend ran into flames. The horror of his screams could be heard for blocks on that otherwise still, balmy, silent night. Inside the blazing apartment the man slams into the wall and falls to the floor. Soon death shall complete the scene, but before death a last struggle with consciousness. Fire engines! He hears fire engines! Hope once again dances across his brow. He'll be saved! He can return to his useless, wasted life.

Church bells, he could hear church bells, but they were somehow different from other church bells he had heard. What was it, what was it that makes these bells different? They're muffled, he realized. It sounds like they're wrapped in burlap or.

. . before he could puzzle out this enigma he died from smoke inhalation.

There is a legend in the French Quarter that whenever there is an outbreak of fire, if one only listens closely, one can hear the manic ringing of muffled church bells emanating from St. Louis Cathedral. It is alleged that this haunting originated Good Friday, 21 March 1788. On that sad night a candle in the private chapel of Don Vincente José Nunez was responsible for a conflagration that raged for over five hours and destroyed 856 buildings (Leavitt, p. 51) and claimed over 1200 dead in a city whose population was 5,338 (H.H.T.). Don Esteban de Miro, the governor, estimated the damage at 2.5 million dollars.

As the fire blossomed, Don Nunez ran two blocks to St. Louis Cathedral so the bells would ring the fire alert. He pounded on the doors and shouted his petition. The good Capuchin fathers under whose authority the cathedral lay heard and then refused Don Nunez's desperate plea. After all, it was Good Friday and to ring the bells on the day of the Savior's death would be an unpardonable blasphemy. If hundreds die then so be it. This is the will of our loving, merciful father, God.

Nunez's heart must have yelled with disgust, "Bull shit!" He and his companions burst into the dark hollow of the church. Their hands found the ropes that snaked upward to the bells. They pulled and pulled. The bells responded with a muffled voice for they had been wrapped with cloth to prevent their inadvertent clamor when assaulted by the irreverent winds. The rest is history.

Ursulines Convent

The Ursulines are an order of Roman Catholic nuns founded at Brescia, Italy in 1535 by Saint Angola Merici. Their mission is directed toward the education of the young — specifically girls and women. Approximately 100 years after their inception one of their convents in the town of Loudun in the province of Pointers, France the good sisters generated a demonic scandal that would 300 years later be chronicled by Aldous Huxley in his book on the subject *The Devils of Loudon* (1952).

The nuns' spiritual welfare was overseen and supervised by Pere Urbain Grandier. By all accounts he was certainly urbane. Handsome. Sophisticated. Liberal. The frustrated, celibate nuns loved him. The Holy Roman Catholic Church despised him. Shortly after assuming his position with the unfulfilled virgins the convent was wracked with demonic hysteria. The prioress, Jean de Agnes and a group of several nuns blamed their hellish lusts and perversions on Father Grandier. The merciful Roman Catholic church arrested him. After a ludicrous, error laden trial Grandier was unrelentlessly tortured and then burned alive (Guiley 1999, pp. 203-206).

It was from this tradition that the Ursulines crawled to New Orleans 7 August 1727 under contract sealed with the Compagnie des Indes previously the Mississippi Company. Their purpose was extraordinarily enlightened for the time. They maintained the city's first "Charity Hospital" open to all individuals residing in the colony regardless of race. Also the good sisters began educating, "...both white and Negro girls the beauties and comforts of religion and to care for the filles á la cassette (whores and female criminals from France) until husbands could be found for them" (Ashbury, p 19).

The nuns also saw to the moral development of their wards as described by a Sister Madeleine, "...by putting them upon wooden horses and having them whipped by the regiment of soldiers that guards the town." (Ibid.) (How charming!)

During the summer outbreaks of yellow fever and malaria the sisters devoted themselves unselfishly to the care of the countless sick and dying. The city fathers showed their gratitude by allowing the Ursulines sisters and the Sisters of Charity to ride public transportation free of charge in perpetuity.

Education was their main stock and trade. Generations of young women were educated by these brides of Christ. To this very day the Ursulines run one of the city's best female educational facilities located at Nashville and Clairborne Avenues.

Ursulines Convent

It should be noted also that the Ursulines Convent which was under construction from 1745 to 1752 is among the oldest existing European structures in the Mississippi Valley. The convent is also one of the few structures in the French Quarter that was actually built by the French. The great conflagrations of 1788 and 1796 virtually eradicated all of the forts, bars, churches, brothels, homes, warehouses and other needful things that had been built by French toil. In actuality 90% of the structures one encounters in the Vieux Carre (Old Quarter) were constructed under Spanish hegemony between 1788 to 1803. From 1802 onward building was under the hegemony of the American Union. In 1936 President Franklin D. Roosevelt's program the WPA rebuilt the French Market and did extensive renovations of many old structures. William Strickland designed and built the United States Mint — erected in 1835. (Huber p. 32). Today the Ursulines Convent serves as the main archives for the Archdiocese of New Orleans, and it is open to visitors.

It would seem that the pious Ursulines have redeemed themselves from the horrors of their past. Devoted nurses. Inspired educators. Dedicated preservationists. All of this points to a group of women who have selflessly dedicated their lives and fortunes to the care and development of their fellow human beings. All of this is done out of a sense of love and charity nurtured within them by their faith in Jesus the Christ, "Our Almighty Savior."

If, on the other hand, we examine their history more carefully and critically we perceive a different occult (concealed/hidden) predicate at work behind the dark skirts of our beloved sisters. You remember Urbain Grandier, the priest/libertine who was so graciously burned at the stake by the Roman Catholic Church? Well, other than Sister Jeanne St. Agnes his chief accuser was one Pere Mignon a Capuchin. Pere Mignon was also the confessor of Father Grandier and betrayed the confidence of the confessional to the Inquisition which condemned Grandier. Mignon then assumed the office of confessor and adviser to these ill fated nuns.

On 6 December 1788 a Capuchin monk. Antonio de Sedella was appointed Commissary of the Inquisition and charged with opening the Holy Office in New Orleans (Ashbury, pp. 54-55). He was also aligned with the spiritual affairs of the Ursulines nuns. The attempt to establish the Inquisition in New Orleans was the only occasion when the monstrous injustice threatened territory that would one day become the United States (Ibid).

Luckily for New Orleans the governor of the city was Don Estevan Miro, an open minded, progressive man who deported Pere de Sedella in the spring in the spring of 1789 and remarked in an official document dated 3 June 1789:

"When I read the communication of that Capuchin, I shuddered. His Majesty has ordered me to foster the increase of population in this province, and to admit in it all those who would emigrate from the banks of these rivers which empty themselves into the Ohio....This emigration was to be encouraged under the pledge that the new colonists should not be molested in matters of religion, provided there should be no other public mode of worship than the Catholic. The mere name of the Inquisition uttered in New Orleans not only would be sufficient to check immigration, which is successfully progressing, but would have recently come, and I fear that, in spite of my having sent out of the country Father Sedella, the most fatal consequences may ensue from the mere suspicion of the cause of his dismissal" (Gayarré's *History of Louisiana*, Volume III, pp. 270-1). In an article in the Louisiana Historical Quarterly for October 1919, Clarence Wyatt Bispham, S.T.M., denied Father Sedella attempted to establish the Inquisition. He maintained that the priest's purposes were purely political.

As further evidence to the dark history of Catholicism in New Orleans I offer this second document:

" . . . Strange things came to light. There were found secret rooms, iron instruments of torture, and other indications that a private court had held meetings there. In addition to this, old newspaper files tell of the discovery of an underground passage which led from the rear of the Cathedral, or from even beyond that point in the direction of the Capuchin monastery — a passage which ended somewhere under the Calaboose. These newspaper accounts are very strange. One day the paper tells of the discovery and promises further disclosures on the following day, when the tunnel has been explored. But it is evident that some pressure was brought to bear on the editor, for there is not a line in any of the later editions of the same paper regarding this discovery. One can only draw his own conclusions" (Gayarré, op. cit.).

de Sedella was appointed head of the Inquisition 6 December 1788. The first fire that destroyed the city flashed to life Good Friday (a Roman Catholic holiday) 21 March (traditional first day of Spring) 1788. Capuchin monks were in charge of St. Louis Cathedral at that time. The Cathedral's bells were muffled that day to prevent their accidental ringing on a holy day dedicated to silence, prayer and fasting. (See the story "Muffled Bells") The originally French built city was almost destroyed totally on that day clearing the decks for a new city of Spanish designed to be fabricated. Interestingly the Ursulines Convent was one of but a handful of French built edifices to survive the fire.

A few years later de Sedella returned as curé of St. Louis Cathedral. Another fire spread through the town 8 December 1794 laying waste to 212 buildings wiping out all but three original French buildings: the Convent of the Ursulines, Madame John's legacy (Dickenson, pp. 52-53) and Lafitte's Blacksmith Shop. The fire also originated on the same block as the first (724 Rue Dumaine/941 Rue Bourbon).

Sealed Shutters

8 December is also a Roman Catholic holy day — the Feast of the Immaculate Conception. Let it be known that the Immaculate Conception is mistakenly identified with the birth of Jesus. (Immaculate Conception, Roman Catholic teaching which, according to the definition (1854) of Pope Pius IX, "maintains that the most blessed Virgin Mary, in the first instant

of her conception, was, by the singular grace and privilege of Almighty God, through the foreseen merits of Christ Jesus the Savior of mankind, preserved immune from all stain of original sin." The doctrine concerns Mary's conception in her mother's womb, and is not to be confused with the virginal conception and birth of Christ.)

Strange, or just simply coincidental, that the Ursulines and Capuchins should be so closely related to such peculiar events which also include collusion with the infamous Inquisition?

The plot deepens. As time flowed on like the murky, mysterious Mississippi strange rumors began to circulate about the old convent. Legend informs us that buried beneath the convent's altar that was constructed in 1845 and known officially as the Chapel of Archbishops are ensconced the preserved hearts of every archbishop who reigned over the archdiocese. When questioned about this peculiar practice the church hierarchy replied with silent disdain (Dickinson, pp. 48-49).

During the 1960's it is alleged that Archbishop Shaw had the eleven shutters on the third floor sealed with 8,000 blessed screws per window. That's 88,000 screws (Ibid). Even for the infamous Roman Catholic Church that's a megalithic screw job! In occult numerology one adds all the numbers in a sequence together to find the base occult signature or idea. 88000=8+8+0+0+0=16=1+6=7. Seven is the number for God. What's being said here?

Larry Montz, internationally recognized parapsychologist, scientist and author of *The Ghosts of New Orleans*, investigated this site. He recorded both objective and subjective responses during his visits to the magnificent building. Obviously he was impressed enough with his results to document his findings and impressions in his book. He gained access to the third floor and found the atmosphere and general environment to be upsetting and unsettling (Montz, pp. 144-145).

It has been alleged that the shuttered attic excited several passers by to report to the police open windows, strange lights and other such occurrences. Upon the arrival and subsequent investigation by the authorities nothing unusual was discovered. The strange events truncated as mysteriously as they appeared (Dickenson, p. 49).

As a final consideration most ghost tours tell stories about the convent being a reservoir for vampires. (See *New Orleans Ghosts II*, pp 104-111 for the *facts* about vampires in the Crescent City). These stories have two points of origin:

1) Ursuline Convent is mentioned in two of Anne Rice's works of fiction *Interview with the Vampire* and *The Witching Hour*.

2) Remember the filles á la Cassette — the French whores and criminals who came here to find husbands *and* redemption? Their nomenclature roughly translates to girls with boxes. All of their possessions were stored in shoe box size cartons which resembled small coffins. These boxes are still stored in the convent. A tour guide of my acquaintance and I discovered them in a 1995 unauthorized inspection of a portion of the building. It is he (R.R.) who started this foolishness.

The Sausage Maker

Generally speaking, body disposal is essential if the felon is to proceed through his life undetected. Sometimes it is advantageous for a body to be found: insurance/estate claims; to send a message, etc. Barring these considerations how and where does one dispose of the most essential evidence–the corpse? If possible disposal should be of such a specie that no body is ever found. No body–no proof of murder.

Certain trades lend themselves to these ends. Incinerator operators, landfill workers, deep sea fishermen are only a few examples of how one can combine his vocational skills with effective, efficient body disposal.

One sterling example comes from the skills and frustration of one Hans Muller, a German immigrant, who plied his trade at 725 Rue Ursulines. Hans and his young wife immigrated to these shores at the turn of the last century. They escaped "the old country" with its traditional virtues of religious intolerance, caste, privilege, poverty. America accepted them with open arms bearing gifts. The greatest bounty the New World bestowed was a unified nation-state based on ideas and principles rather than traditions.

Anyway, Hans and his wife opened a butcher's shop which soon became well known for its hearty, delectable sausages. Hans brought his trade to the Crescent City where he began to mingle Creole and Cajun spices with his rich pork, beef and blood sausages. The price of success is hard work. Hans thrived as did his business but his wife fared differently. The stress of a new country, the hard work, and, yes, the never-ending suspicions about her husband aged her well beyond her comparatively young age.   The sausages and heavy beer created creases where there were once curves.

Hans was a popular man in a city that lives and loves to eat and drink. Hans' knowledge of the preparation of the meats and meat products he prepared combined with a magnanimous, if sometimes boisterous, personality drew him many admirers—especially female. After all, he brought his wife to the new world; she was well provided for, she certainly had plenty to eat and drink. Their sex life, once a raging river, had devolved into a drought raped creek. "What, *mine Himmel*, should she expect of me?", he must have rationalized.

He was a man—a prosperous tradesman—with needs and desires that had become alien to her. They worked together. They lived together. A man needs attention or diversity or maybe just understanding. So what if he had a roving eye? He was a man, and, yes men are Pigs but women are Bitches.

As business boomed Hans decided it was time for an employee who could wrap his wares and clean his block and knives and run errands and by her presence convey the image of success so important to success. He hired Ilse. She was also German. Her skin was smooth like the surface of cream. She had glacial blue eyes draped by hair that reminded him of thick, sun drenched summer's wheat. Ilse's body was a series of firm curves which convinced our amorous meat cutter of her obvious proclivity with arithmetic which is a great asset for a shop clerk. She was hired immediately.

Mrs. Muller was at first pleased with the affable Fraulein. She was honest, clean and more importantly her bucolic, fresh good looks and somewhat flirtatious manner brought more men to the shop which meant more money. Hans and she could also have more quality time since Ilse's efficiency gave them more time to be together by lessening their collective work load.

As winter beckoned spring, Mrs. Muller's suspicions blossomed. Hans seemed to touch Ilse an awful lot. There was something more than "friendly" in their smiles. It was obvious. She knew it . . . felt it. Hans was giving his affections to Ilse.

It all started innocently enough. Sure, Hans was attracted to his charming new clerk but what man wouldn't be? Soon he found himself fantasizing about her and fantasizing about her fantasizing about him. One cool, bright spring evening he suddenly realized his erection could be detected beneath his bloody apron. Did his wife notice? She did–he knew it–by her eyes and her frown–she knew. Hell, if a man's going to hang he just as well be guilty as not. It was then he decided to try to bed the Tyrolean Tart. He succeeded.

Their stolen hours of love launched him on the raging river of passion once again. He felt alive. He was attractive, wanted, virile and loved by Ilse. Money poured into the shop. Life was good.

Frau Muller could not endure this peccadillo. Not under her very nose. She would confront him this very night as soon as he returned home from some "urgent deliveries." She waited in the darkened shop. Thoughts of Hans and Ilse bore obscene holes in her imagination. She could see his kissing her lips, her breasts, the thoughts repelled her but she could not stop them from writhing before her mind's eye. In a perverse way these images not only repelled her but brought her a kind of penance. She realized that she had grown fat. She realized that her ardor for her beloved Hans had waned. For this she felt guilt. Her guilt punished her.

Hans was home. His footsteps were heavy on the worn, wooden steps. He didn't see her in the dark recesses of the shop where she had been sobbing silently. "Hans," she cried, "*wie geht's*"?

"*Mein Gott*," he spat out in surprise.

She smelled beer on his breath and perfume and the smell of Ilse's body and oh, God damn it, she smelled their fuck!

He moved toward her hypnotized, Beer, love, lies, sex, frustration (Kirk p. 5) numbed him to her invective; her indictments. Her words chiseled into the frigid ice stone of his gut/heart. The harsh, guttural German words of her indictments slashed through her ears and oozed into his throbbing brain. He stumbled backward from the force of her words and her hurt, angered eyes. He began to fall. He reached out for support. His hand felt a familiar shape. It was the meat cleaver so familiar to him as an essential tool of his trade. In a blinding instant it was in his hand traveling toward her skull. Again and again and again the seasoned steel found its mark. His wife fell. Unconsciousness embraced the butcher. As the orange claws of dawn shredded the darkness of the shop consciousness invaded Hans' unthinking mind. His eyes relayed the message of his environment to our hapless felon's brain. His wife lay before him in a wilderness of blood, bone and mangled brains. "What have I done, what have I done?" his mind echoed into the abyss of his guilt born fear.

"I'll die at the end of a rope, oh, God help me, forgive me," he muttered in confused desperation.

His mind cleared. A plan formulated and he began its implementation immediately. Hans drew the curtains, placed a closed sign in the window, and began the process of erasing the evidence of his crime. He stripped his wife and began to clean and dress her as he had done so many times to thousands of anonymous hogs and cattle. As he labored he reflected that the blood and bones presented no real problem for him—a Metzner—a butcher. After all, bones and blood were common in his trade. Soon his wife would simply be a hundred kilos or so of sausage. Within a few hours the task was done. The sausage was piled high on a enamel platter. The shop was cleaned. He burned her blood drenched clothes and bathed.

The following morning he opened his shop as was his custom. When asked about his closing the previous day and his distraught demeanor, he replied that his wife had left him to return to Germany. The story was plausible. There was no reason for doubt. He and Ilse could now pursue their love without hindrance. Oh, yes, his new sausages were a great hit. The customers loved them.

Nevertheless, all was not well. The guilt Hans experienced became a ravenous deamon that manifested itself in hallucinations and madness akin to Poe's "Telltale Heart." His wife's face was everywhere. Her voice rang through the air as the unrelenting bells of Beelzebub accusing him, bearing witness against him, tormenting him. Making love was impossible. Work was impossible. Life impossible. He retreated into his upstairs rooms. Closed his shop. Ilse left. Hans became a recluse. Soon after that a customer was enjoying one of Hans's delectable sausages. He bit down on a hard object. It was a gold wedding ring. Dissecting the sausage he discovered a fingernail. After a bout of vomiting he called the police who immediately called upon Hans. They found that the affable butcher had become a disoriented mad man. He was committed to an insane asylum (ibid, pp. 85-86).

His shop passed through a succession of proprietors. None stayed. Each reported eerie noises and on occasion a bloody, mutilated female screaming about infidelity. This haunting continued until Hans took his life.

One final note. I began this tale by addressing the necessity of body disposal if one is going to succeed at murder. I address this issue as a writer, not necessarily a practitioner, and herein enter a disclaimer saying that the facts I articulate are presented as entertainment only.

When disposing of a body through burial, the following practices should be observed:

1. Never wrap a body in plastic or any other material for it retards decay.

2. Bury the body nude—no clothing, jewelry, etc. for such artifacts contribute to identification.

3. Remove the teeth. If you wait at least four hours there will be minimum blood. Dispose of the teeth one by one while driving on the interstate, or some other well traveled road.

4. Crush the skull and pour H_2SO_4 on it. Wait for acid to work. This retards forensic reconstruction if your "work" is some day discovered.

5. DNA can only identify a body if it can be compared to the deceased's relatives. If the identity of the victim cannot be ascertained then it is impossible to find such.

6. If the police do surface you as a suspect in either a disappearance or murder politely but firmly advise them that your attorney has advised you to never allow yourself to be questioned by the police unless he/she is present. Admit nothing. Deny nothing. Say only what is above advised. It is better for the police to think you are guilty than to be found guilty by a court. Remember, more murderers have ended up on the end of a rope as a consequence of their own mouths than by effective police work. The cops are fishermen who can only

score a catch if the fish (suspect) opens his mouth and swallows the hook. Cops are infamous liars. Protect your rights.

7. Clean up blood with a strong solution of boric acid, followed with chlorine bleach, followed by another boric acid rinse.

8. If it is necessary to dissect the body never cut through joints. For instance cut below or above the knee, ankle, etc. Cutting through joints is a real pain in the ass.

9. *Always* pay attention to details!

If cremating or disposing of a body in water follow the above with these subject specific activities:

1. Cremation – spread the ashes over as large an area as possible. This allows the remains to blend into the environment and not standout.

2. Burial at sea – (a) Weigh the body down with common materials available everywhere. (b) Open all body cavities with axe or knife. These cavities will fill with gas and the buoyance will overcome almost any reasonable weight. The body will bob to the surface and more than likely be found. Always remember no body–no evidence of murder.

The Shadow of Compte de Saint Germain

New Orleans has been associated with a mismatched and bizarre cast of characters in its almost three hundred years of history. De La Salle, Iberville, John Law, Louis XIV, Jefferson, Napoleon, Andrew Jackson, P.G.T. Beauregard, Lefcadio Hern, Aleister Crowley, Lee Harvey Oswald, Anne Rice, Victor C. Klein among thousands of other luminaries and lunatics have all left fingerprints on this mystical, magical crescent that oozes between Lake Pontchartrain and the Mississippi River.

Our concern is with the eldritch, the bizarre, the arcane. In that vein we are going to examine the strange story of Compte de Saint Germain born circa 1700 - died unknown. His exact date and place of birth are unknown; however, he enters into the historical record in 1745 when he was accused of espionage. Horace Walpole vouched for him and he was known personally by a variety of luminaries of XVIII century Europe including Louis XV, Madame de Pompadour, Casanova, the Grimm Brothers, Saint-Martin and a host of others (Sadoul, pp. 189-191).

His name was associated with an array of secret societies: Rose-Croix, the *Illuminati*, the *Cabalists*, the Humanitarians and the Free Masons (Ibid, 192).

He told fantastic tales about having known King Solomon and Jesus. The Compte also related that he possessed the elixir of life and could transmute base metals into gold and create perfect diamonds. He was never known to eat or drink in public and held no interest in sexual activity of any kind. Saint-Germaine was fluent in many languages and displayed an encyclopedic knowledge. Everyone he met was impressed by his personality. In 1794 his death was reported but he allegedly surfaced on occasion after this time (Ibid., 189 ff).

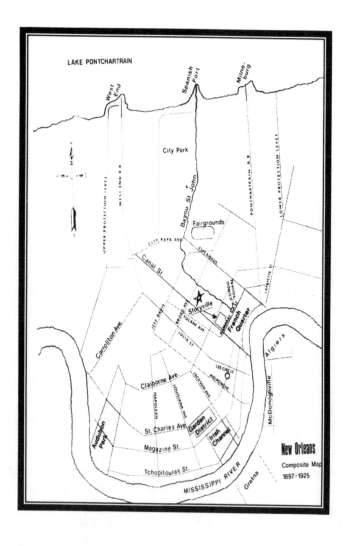

Storyville Map 1897-1925

Many legends grew around this individual including that he was immortal, that he was a deity, a priest, possibly a vampire. (Spence p. 345). His name is widely known in occult and esoteric literature. Many books and monographs have been written about his exploits and abilities. The man, whoever he was, generates interest to this day.

At the turn of the twentieth century an individual came to New Orleans and rented a house in the French Quarter. This person was obviously a man of means for he had the ability to live well with no visible means of support. Little was known of him except that he revealed he was from the south of France and that his name was Jacques St. Germain. He also claimed to be a descendant of our illustrious Compte. (Smith, p. 138).

Jacques lived quietly and drew little attention to himself until one night in 1903. During this time period prostitution was legalized and confined to a particular area of the city just outside the French Quarter and referred to as Storyville. (Rose, pp 1-4. See map.) Prostitution, then, as now, can be a dangerous occupation. Legalization lessens the dangers of disease, exploitation and violence but, none the less prostitutes have commerce with that most vicious and cunning of animals — man!

On the night in question Jacques went "cruising". He met her— "Helena" — in one of the city's many absinthe bars. He caught her eye immediately. Handsome, finely dressed and well manicured Jacques was a whore's dream come true. No unkempt, smelly brute was this, but a gentleman with fine manners and a romantic French accent that was not the local Creole patois. His French was continental and suggested an excellent education and breeding. (It should be remarked that the French language did not die out in Vieux Carre until the "Depression" of the 1930's). Soon she found herself accompanying him to his home. Upon entering she felt something was wrong. The abode was dark and heavy with the smell of incense. She also sensed the smell of death. Fear began to clear her head of the effects of the Absinthe and not a second too soon. The handsome gentleman was on top of her sinking his teeth — no his fangs — into her throat. She struggled against his lethal embrace but his strength was overwhelming. With one last burst of fear propelled panic her knee met his testicles. His grip loosened. She bolted for the dark street and freedom. She ran. He did not follow. Somehow she found the police and related her story as well as she could. The cops brought her to Charity Hospital where she soon died (Smith, p. 138).

The authorities descended on Saint Germain's home. He was no where to be found; however, the walls and floors were caked with blood and gore — some fresh — some old. No bodies were uncovered. Saint Germain disappeared (Ibid.)

Was this the figure of legend? Who knows? But, after all, is this not the substance of which legends are made?

The Morgue

From behind the bar a skull grins. A crime scene outline of a murdered body is sketched on the floor beside the pool table. A coal black cat named mouse passively surveys the scene from the top of a nineteenth century coffin. All around the dark interior are scattered implemetia of the cemetery: funeral urns, crucifixes, decaying funeral wreaths faded with age and neglect contribute to the eldritch miasmic effluvia that weighs in the atmosphere like the stillness of death. Bartenders' Magazine, spring 2002.

Is this the home of some psychotic deviant, or the set of a John Carpenter film? Neither. It is the interior of a bar–The Morgue. This bar is on the ground floor of a nearly 200-year-old two-story brick structure built in the Spanish colonial style. A city survey of 1836 indicates that at that time it was used as a stable. Shortly after that, it was used as a morgue to accommodate the countless victims of yellow fever, malaria, typhoid, typhus, syphilis, murder and mayhem who breathed their last in this city embraced by the crescent of the Mississippi River.

From its founding in 1718, New Orleans was one of the most unhealthy cities in North America. The climate is semi-tropical. Water surrounds the city, and more often than not the metropolis' frequent rains that bathe the city cause an almost permanent state of flood. High humidity and New Orleans' seven-foot mean below sea level contribute to boglike conditions that are breeding grounds for the most dangerous animals known to humanity – Anopheles and Aedes aegypti the disease carrying mosquitoes which have been responsible for more human deaths than any other organism. This harbinger of human disaster is the medium through which a panopole of diseases are transmitted. When you add human habitation to this mix, one finds garbage and sewerage which adds to and encourages the various local pathogens.

It has been estimated that as much as 15% of the city's population died annually as a result of the various epidemics that sliced through the town like the Grim Reaper's scythe. Storing and preparing the deceased was a megalithic, and given the damp, hot climate, repulsive task.

Ghosts Outside of The Morgue
(Luminous bottom center)

The building at 626 rue St. Philip served as a morgue for the city during the early period in its history. It should also be noted that bodies were stored and prepared here regardless of race. This is remarkable because discrimination was maintained even in death. Many of our cemeteries exhibit this reality in that there is a white section and a "colored" section. Even in death the Negro was denied equality under the law.

Enterprises and businesses came and went at the St. Philip address. In more recent years a number of bars and cabarets entertained our raucous citizens. I became acquainted with the bar in May 2001 when I entered into an agreement with Mr. Don Becker to sell my books in conjunction with his tour appropriately named "New Orleans Ghost Tour" see Appendix). I might also add that of all of the ghost tours that have come into existence because of my work, he was the only individual to extend the courtesy of allowing me to sell my books and share in the profits of this most lucrative endeavor. For this he has my eternal respect and gratitude. Once again, thank you, Don.

Not only did my book sales escalate, it was part of our agreement that I could drink free and the chances of my being beaten into insensibility and thrown into the gutter or worse a jail cell were virtually non-existent. I also met scores of attractive women with out-of-town drivers' licenses, who were more than willing to have a romp in the hay with a handsome, charming, modest genius who wrote books. What a great life–DWI's not withstanding. During my tenure at "The Morgue" I became aware of the fact that it was most definitely haunted. Several of the bartenders had told me strange stories about the place, particularly the women's lavatory. I took these stories with a grain of salt until several female patrons began relating bizarre stories about their experiences in the bathroom. The accounts are too numerous to mention individually; however, one sticks in my mind and is emblematic of the rest. While waiting for the tour to begin, I struck up a conversation with a raven-haired beauty from Austin, Texas. After about ten minutes, she excused herself to "power her nose." When she returned, she was visibly shaken. This is what she related.

"I went to the bathroom and entered the stall and closed the door. Not more than fifteen seconds someone seemed to push the door. I said, 'Someone's in here, hun.' Three or four seconds later it happened again. I said, 'Hey, I'm in here, O.K.'? Again, a couple of seconds later, guess what, it happens a third time. I got pissed and opened the door. You know what? Nobody's there! Suddenly the stall door slams and the lock fell into place without me touching it or anything. Spooky, huh?" (Kalila Smith relates similar stories in her book *Journey into Darkness*, p. 94).

This is not the end of it. One day, Don Becker made an addition to the decor. He put a small (about two feet long, ten inch wide) coffin behind the bar. In the coffin, he placed a doll circa 1850's, some moss and a wooden crucifix. From that day on weird things began to happen. The toilet in the men's room began to back up on a daily basis. Plumbers came and went. The problem remained.   First one, then the second air conditioner failed. The refrigeration unit behind the bar failed. It was repaired. It failed again. It was replaced only to have the replacement fail. Vandalism was suspected.   Sabotage investigated. No rational cause could be surfaced. Then it was recognized that all of these events began on the very day the coffin and doll made their debut. The coffin and its occupant were removed. The negative phenomena ceased immediately.

April 18, 2002

Mr. Klein,

On a visit to New Orleans on April 6th my daughter & I took the Ghost Tour that leaves from the Morgue bar on St. Philip St. I also purchased both of your books which you signed for me.

I thought these two photos might interest you; they were taken before the tour, or reading your books.

Sincerely,
Joan Duva
5201 SW 31 Ave
Daniu, FL 33312

**More French Quarter Ghosts
(Luminous shoulder, up and left)**

Arnaud's Restaurant

A rnaud's Restaurant is among the finest in a city known for extraordinary dining. Shrimp Arnaud and Red Fish filet with lump crabmeat hollandaise are internationally renowned. Begun in 1920 by Arnaud Cazenave the establishment was unique because it thrived and became famous under the hand of a female chef, Madame Pierre.

After Cazenave's death the establishment was operated by his daughter, Germaine Cazenave Wells. She not only established a reputation for herself as a restaurateur, but as a singer of acclaim. She maintained direct control until the 1970's when she leased the business to outside interests (Cowen, et al., p. 206).

Apart from fantastic fare and bountiful beverages the place is haunted. In my extensive and exhaustive researches about local hauntings I have found no documentation of this site and only a cursory mention of having been investigated as a haunted environment. The citation was in Larry Montz's tome *ISPR Investigates the Ghosts of New Orleans*, p 160. The only information he provides is that Arnaud's was investigated by his team.

I became aware of the potential for a story when in the Fall of 1993 I appeared as a guest on a local T.V. program *The Angela Hill Show*, hosted by local television personality Angela Hill of WWL Channel Four. There were several guests on the show including Larry Montz. This is where I first met him and became aware of another fellow traveler. The other guest who caught my interest was an employee of the establishment in question for over thirty years. I cannot supply his name because as of this writing I have been unable to surface the tape of the show either in my records or that of the stations. Calling Arnaud's provided no help in that they were interested in reservations and not the ramblings of a somewhat eccentric occult writer. As a result of these misfortunes this will be a somewhat skeletal story based on my memory and a few scant notes.

There is no apparent etiology for the manifestation to be described, i.e. no sour love affairs, tragic demises, or black magick of which I am aware. The hauntings are most common and noticeable in the wine cellar where wait staff have reported spectral assaults such as being touched by unseen hands or hearing the sound of breath from invisible entities. They have also reported a generalized eerie feeling when retrieving vino for guests. There have also surfaced reports of psychokinetic activities. The table settings have been disrupted. Silverware, china, napkins and place settings have been, in some instances reduced to chaos. How valid are these stories I cannot say.

There is only one thing of which I am convinced absolutely. If you are fortunate enough to dine at Arnaud's your experience will be celestial.

Napoleon's Refuge

N apoleon was one of the most influential individuals of the last millennium. Not only was he a brilliant general, but a true visionary. Long before the advent of the European Union Bonaparte conceptualized a unified Europe founded on the principles of democracy, liberty and fraternity encouraged and supported by scientific ideas and not the superstitions of the tyranny of religion.

The Refuge of Mayors and Emperors

This genius was responsible for laws based on reason — the Napoleonic Code. He launched the discipline of Egyptology and in so doing married the scientific method of Descartes with history. Napoleon was a seminal thinker in urban planning. He created our modern system of street addresses with even and odd numbers on alternate sides of a thoroughfare.

All of these accolades were diminished because of the Emperor's tragic flaw of the need for absolute power. He ruled as an absolute monarch and carried nepotism into the arms of excessive absurdity. Never the less, he left an indelible mark upon history.

Napoleon House Restaurant and National Historic Landmark

The Napoleon House Restaurant began serving patrons in 1914. The building from which it operates was erected in 1797; however, fire and reconstruction and renovation propels the actual date of its present form to 1814. This site served as the residence of one of the Crescent City's many colorful mayors Nicholas Girod (Montz, p. 86).

Girod was the mayor of the city when the Battle of New Orleans was fought 8 January 1814. Andrew Jackson with a motley, ill-armed and trained ragtag army of 3,100 combatants met a force of 7,500 seasoned British regulars under the command of General Sir Edward Pakenham. When the smoke cleared Pakenham and two of his senior officers were dead along with 2,100 of his troops. This was the last battle of the War of 1812. Ironically the conflict took place after the Treaty of Ghent was signed ending the war. The results of this battle were manifold:

1. British Colonial ambitions were effectively at an end in North America.

2. It unified the United States and reaffirmed its revolution.

3. It secured the Mississippi Valley.

4.The United States was developing into world power independent of any European control.

5. Andrew Jackson became president of the United States and moved the country into an arena of greater freedom as expressed by Jacksonian democracy (Leavitt, p. 76.).

Mayor Girod Offers Refuge

Nicholas Girod was an American by the chance of history. Ultimately he saw himself as foremost a Creole — a person of French or Spanish heritage born in the New World. As such he hated the English and loved all things French. That love was especially extended to Napoleon Bonaparte. The French emperor had transformed France into one of the most powerful nations in the world. He also espoused a philosophy based on human dignity, freedom and liberty.

When Napoleon escaped from his exile on Elba Nicholas Gird and his brother Claude Pierre announced their intention to provide the Little Corporal with refuge in the mansion they owned in New Orleans. Napoleon attempted to seek asylum in the U.S.; however, his plan did not come to fruition and again he pursued his military adventures only to find defeat at Waterloo 100 days after his escape from Elba. This time Bonaparte was delivered to remote St. Helena in the vast expanses of the Atlantic Ocean.

Even this grim reality did not dampen the desires of the Girod brothers to liberate Napoleon and deliver him to the Crescent City. They created a syndicate of wealthy supporters who purchased the schooner *Seraphine* — allegedly one of the world's fastest ships. They hired the mercenary pirate and hero of the Battle of New Orleans Jean Lafitte and his cutthroats to pilot the ship and executed the mission. Before Napoleon could be rescued he died, and so did the expedition (Ibid, p 77).

The Napoleon House still stands and by its very name maintains the legend as well as something else. It is a bona fide haunted edifice. Larry Montz, Ph.D. is one of the most respected and professional paranormal investigators in the world. He was invited to examine the site after many people had reported peculiar events. Bartenders reported bottles and *implementia* moved by no earthly hand. A man who appeared to be a Confederate soldier was seen and then suddenly disappeared. An older African-American woman was also reported to haunt the restaurant as well.

After exhaustive research Dr. Montz concluded that the hauntings were valid according to his objective and subjective criteria. I recommend the Napoleon House to everyone interested in history, ambiance, great food and drink and the desire to experience the possibility of a ghostly meeting.

The Secret in the Garden

S ex, murder, guilt, suicide — this story has it all. In 1789 the building now housing O' Flaherty's Irish Pub was constructed (Montz, p. 91). The old structure was owned by one Joseph Bapentier in the first few years of the nineteenth century. He was a prosperous merchant whose feed and grain store occupied the first floor of the building. He resided on the second and third floors. Joseph prospered with the American purchase of Louisiana. A stable government based on republican principles and an agriculturally based economy joined to the mighty Mississippi River and Gulf of Mexico made the bejeweled city at the river's mouth among the wealthiest and most sophisticated on the globe.

Our merchant prospered. In 1806 during the month of October he elected to marry Mary Wheaton, a native of Cumberland, New Jersey. This was a shrewd move. As an American of Anglo-Saxon descent she provided a much needed cultural bridge for the Creole businessman. At first the marriage went well. There were balls and masques. Great food, fine beverages and a balmy climate contributed to their lovemaking, to their happiness.

On the surface everything appeared perfect. On the surface, that is. As a Creole — a Frenchman — with Latin blood and passions Joseph engaged in the time honored practice of *placage*. This custom dictated that a married man was free to take a mistress to as along as he was discreet and supported her. Joseph, being a gentleman who appreciated and seconded cultural values participated in the custom. He acquired a beautiful French damsel whose name was Angelique. The name befitted her for she was an angel to him. While he loved his wife Mary the Anglo-Saxon transplant did not bring to the marriage bed the joys, pleasures and passions that his Latin lover shared with him. The world in which he found himself was perfect. Money poured in from his lucrative business. His wife was a refined American who eased his culture shock from a Spanish colony to an American state. And, oh yes, he had the sensual beauty of his Seraphim Angelique. Life was great.

Alas, soon our protagonist would be driven from paradise by the very angel he worshiped. His "babe", his beauty began to demand more money, more time, more of his soul lest she inform his somewhat puritanical, parochial Mary of their love. He faced devastation and humiliation.

"Mon Dieux, Non!", his mind screamed in the clouded recesses of his reason.

He struggled with the daemon given birth by Angelique's selfish demands. As he assumed the role of Jacob and wrestled with the Angel of Betrayal, Angelique strode into the store. She repeated her demands. They were alone. He locked the doors; drew the curtains. Anger exploded as a red cloud of venom. His powerful, tradesman's hand grabbed for her delicate throat. The Whore of Babylon heard the thunderous hoof beats of the Pale Rider coming to bestow on her the reward of death. She found temporary escape on the stairs ascending heavenward. She ran. He followed. She screamed. He cursed. On the second floor her ascent found terminus. Joseph's hands found justice, vengeance. He repaid her arrogance by launching her through a window. Angelique's head crashed onto the paved courtyard. Her skull was crushed; her neck broken. She instantly fell into the embrace of Azrael — the Angel of the West — the Angel of Death.

The shop keeper ran down the stairs. The crime must be hidden — obscured. In the patio was a sewer opening. Joseph grabbed the body and threw it into the reeking, black hole. The evidence was gone — he was safe. Almost as soon as comfort began to caress his feverish mind he detected a noise. It was Nehemiah — his young slave boy. The boy ran in panic.

Guilt and fear quickly evicted the comfort that had soothed his consciousness. He knew what would happen when the boy returned with the authorities. Preempting the judicial process he acquired a length of hemp rope, retired to the third floor and hanged himself without delay.

Mary inherited the house. She died in 1817 a the age of 35. She left no heirs (Ibid. 94.)

Today the home is occupied by O' Flaherty's Irish Channel Pub. It is a great bar in a city of great bars. It is also a very "spirited" place.

The owner Danny O' Flaherty became aware early on that his bar not only served spirits but was serviced by them as well. After a host of inexplicable occurrences he had his building investigated based on three unanswered questions.

"Who was the woman on the balcony, why were his employees so frightened, and why were there old security bars on the third floor?" (ibid p. 91.)

Many customers observed a lone, silent woman peering from the balcony. She seemed to enjoy the great live music that is featured on a nightly basis. Being a true man of the sod and a romantic Danny O' Flaherty composed a ballad for his spectral audience of one. She seemed to appreciate his efforts.

His employees have also experienced an interesting species of events. On occasion workers at the pub who exhibited behavior that was unacceptable to our shade (it is presumed to be Mary) would be battered by shoves and pushes from invisible hands.

The pub also served as a rendezvous for a nightly ghost tour that met in the courtyard for a preliminary round of refreshments. More than one participant experienced an eerie coldness and presence especially if they stood by the old, sealed well. No one was aware of the cavern's existence or history before the tour. Young men and children reported being caressed by an ingenue who promptly disappeared when eye contact was made. After the tour these occurrences began to make sense to the participants.

The origin of the security bars on the third floor remain a mystery. Are they designed to keep out a burglar with a ladder; or, more ominously, to keep something in?

Before O' Flaherty's acquired the place he heard of a Voodoo ritual that was performed in 1987 to quite the ghosts. Apparently, it didn't work.

This site is well documented and very active (see Bibliography for *Historic New Orleans Collection* as well as Montz and Smith).

Paranormal experiences defy quantitative articulation. As such they are considered random events. Skeptics will deny even this (see *New Orleans Ghosts I*, pp. 107-114). One thing this author will guarantee is that if you find yourself at this pub you will find great food and drink in an entertaining, friendly atmosphere.

Courthouse Revenants

Gunshots thunder against the marble halls of justice located in New Orleans' historic *Vieux Carre*. A neatly dressed Afro-American gentleman lies mortally wounded on the hard, cold floor. A few meters away a Caucasian woman breathes her last in an ever expanding pool of crimson. They lost their lives because they dared to testify against the infamous, deadly *Cosa Nostra* that once controlled so much of the vice *and* legal pursuits of the Crescent City.

The time was the 1930's. New Orleans was corrupt and corrupting. Gambling and liquor were illegal. So were prostitution and narcotics. Whenever governments act against human nature by trying to outlaw natural human impulses and desires chaos, crime and destruction follow. So it was in the America of the 1930's, and so it is today. Do they never learn?

No more editorializing. Occupying one square block in the French Quarter bounded by rues Charters, Royal, St. Louis and Conti this imposing building began dispensing justice from 1909 to 1964. From 1964 until the 1990's it served as the Wildlife and Fisheries Museum. In the 1990's extensive renovations were begun to refurbish and restore the splendid structure (Montz, p. 17.). It was during this period that I became aware of rumors concerning this locale's being haunted. I proceeded to investigate. I was accompanied by Mary Milan — a.k.a. Bloody Mary who operates a colorful tour in the French Quarter. We arrived around noon. The construction workers were at lunch.

We planned our research so that we could have interviews that would not interfere with the work. We spoke with a supervisor and several workers, all of whom agreed to speak with us on the condition of anonymity. Each man related different stories about tools and materials being misplaced. One individual, an electrician, explained the great difficulties he had with the wiring. He said he anticipated a degree of electrical problems because it was an old building in a hot, humid climate; however, his anticipations paled to the reality of the situation. There were constant power problems despite new wiring, double insulations and above code groundings. He declared it was the most frustrating and difficult job for which he had ever contracted in twenty-eight years of electrical work.

Spirits of Justice

Although each man had a different story they all related a startlingly similar tale about a well dressed, middle age, white gentleman whom they individually confronted looking out of an upper story window. The peculiar aspect of these encounters was that the man would "vanish into thin air" literally.

As of this writing (15 May 2004) construction on the old courthouse has been suspended due to over expenditures and a corresponding lack of funds. Interestingly enough guests at the Omni Royal Orleans (Also a haunted site, see *New Orleans Ghosts II*, p. 10.) directly across the street from the vacant building call the front desk on a continual basis to complain about a middle age man who stands motionless and stares into their rooms with an intense visage. The clerks are so used to these complaints that they have a stock answer. They informed the concerned guests that the man is an attorney who has engaged in this practice for years. He is simply meditating on his legal work and is an established gentleman of impeccable credentials who means no harm. What they fail to mention is that the building in question is deserted, and that yes the man in question was an attorney from the 1920's until his death in the late 1950's (Stewart, p. 11).

Gay Ghosts

In the story "The Morgue", I spoke of a cat named mouse. Now it is appropriate for me to introduce you to her mistress — Angel Rivero. This is an extraordinary woman of Gypsy and Apache descent. She is a woman with a mane of raven black traces that fall to her taut waist. She and I became lovers. We remain friends as of this writing. When she became aware of the fact that I was writing yet another *New Orleans Ghosts* book she said, "Hey, Daddy, your books are great, but you've failed to included any gay sites in them. C'mon, man, San Francisco, Key West, New York, New Orleans are all gay Meccas. How come you got no gay sites, huh?"

To which I replied in classical *Naw'luns patois*, "Yea, ya rite! What ya got fur me, baby?"

It was at this point that she informed me of "The Round Up". Angel is a New York transplant who has developed herself into a French Quarter personality. She is known by virtually everyone who lives and works in this unique community. She has been a tour guide, bartender, model promoter, but most of all she brings joy into almost every life she touches because of her humor and love for life and living.

"The Round Up" is located in a building that dates back from the 1850's. It is one of the oldest gay bars in the city dating to at least the 1940's when it was owned by a boisterous, garrulous woman affectionately known as "Mom". During this period the bar had a reputation for being a tough, *rough trade* bar that catered to seamen, biker types and macho leather guys. Today, while still a gay bar its clientele is very diverse. Drag queens, transgender persons, regular gay guys as well as a surprising number of women were in and out while I was doing interviews, taking pictures and, of course, having a few cocktails.

Old Club Entrance

I was informed by George Simmons, the manager that the pub could boast of famous patrons including Tennessee Williams, Truman Capote and Rock Hudson. It was also the hangout of Clay Shaw prominent New Orleans business person, and a key player in Jim Garrison's investigation into the New Orleans connection in regards to the assassination of President John F. Kennedy. The reader will recall that Lee Harvey Oswald Kennedy's alleged assassin, was born and reared in New

Orleans. Also, Jack Ruby (Rubenstein) had business concerns, and a home in our fair city.

The bar experienced its share of violence, passion and intrigue. The haunting activity here is as diverse and eclectic as its history and clientele. Mr. Simmons related a variety of inexplicable happenings. In its early days, "Mom" had quarters on the second floor. Here she would drink and entertain various friends of both genders. On occasion things would get out of hand and when they did Mom was not shy about cracking a few skulls and sometimes speaking through the barrel of one of her several pistols. To this day the management and patrons report hearing the sounds of violent confrontation issuing from these unoccupied rooms.

Psychokinesis is also commonplace. Liquor bottles, glasses and bar implements are constantly changing positions. No mundane hand of flesh and bone is responsible for such disturbances. They have been going on for decades.

Lights of unknown origin also appear and disappear. Sometimes the luminescence is accompanied by weird sounds. Sometimes they are not.

Whether you are gay or not you owe yourself a trip to this interesting bar. You will be entertained. You could be shocked. You might experience a ghost!

San Francisco Plantation

The Antebellum South's economy was based on the plantation system and the individuals who owned the expansive agricultural investments were the aristocracy of the region. Such was Valsin Marmillion who in 1849 began construction of one of the most beautiful mansions to grace the banks of the mighty Mississippi. His home is designed to resemble a steamboat. It is a plastered brick, three story home with wide galleries that mirror the double decks of the romantic boats that at one time dominated river trade and traffic.

As fate would dictate Valsin Marmillion did not live to see his plantation house completed. He experienced a financial drain as a consequence of his great expenditure in constructing the edifice. His health failed and he died. Shortly before his death he called his house San Fruscin which in the French slang of the time meant "my last red cent" (Laughlin p. 79.) The name stuck and was corrupted into San Francisco which it will be forever known.

After Valsin's death the house passed to his German born wife and his three sons Pierre, Antoine and Charles. In 1870 Antoine and Charles bought out the other heirs and remained in residence until their untimely deaths in 1871 and 1875 respectively.

Tragedy followed the two Marmillion heirs in that Antoine lost his two year old daughter when, while playing she tumbled down the stairs and was killed. Her older brother fared no better. He fell into a sugar bin and suffocated (Smith p. 115).

The plantation passed to Charles who was also followed by misfortune. He died in 1875 from congenital syphilis. San Francisco Plantation then went through a succession of owners until its being assumed by the San Francisco Plantation Foundation. The foundation has restored and preserved it. It is open to tours. Officers of the foundation have on at two least separate occasions requested that the house be examined by paranormal investigators.

One team was led by renowned parapsychologist Larry Montz, Ph.D. The other group was directed by Kalia Katherina Smith a local author and co-founder of Haunted History Tours. While neither group was aware of the others' findings they both reported almost identical information and experiences. There were significant electromagnetic fields in the attic and several rooms that were used as offices by Charles Marmillion. Also, classical cold spots were found in the same locations.

The investigations were instigated because employees of the plantation foundation had on numerous occasions heard children laughing and playing in the attic when no children — at lease live children — were present. Also, a young bearded man smoking a cigar was witnessed walking around the house. The man was Charles Marmillion. A cigar smoker in his life as well as in death.

This is a very active haunting that has been going on regularly for well over one hundred years.

Haunted Saints

I t's a Sunday afternoon. The New Orleans Saints are playing the Atlanta Falcons in the Louisiana Superdome. There are no timeouts and only twelve seconds left on the clock. The Saints have possession and are leading 25 to 20. The quarterback receives the ball. As he steps back to fall on the pigskin it inexplicably shoots straight up out of his hands. A defensive tackle grabs the airborne ball and lumbers all the way for a touchdown. The Saints lose 26 to 25. Yet again the Saints have snatched defeat from the jaws of victory.

Since the franchise began almost forty years ago the Saints have established themselves as one of the worst teams in the NFL. They have changed managers, coaches, quarterbacks, strategies, even owners and nothing has abated their continual, dismal record.

What explains their monumental bad luck? Someone once remarked that if you transposed the Dallas Cowboys to New Orleans and the Saints to Dallas the Saints would win the Super Bowl and the Cowboys would assume the Saints' dubious distinction of being among the worst teams in the NFL. The commentator who framed this remark explained that the reason for this is the miasmic effluvia which has permeated the city since its founding in 1718. This miasmic effluvia finds expression in the city's carefree, decadent approach to life. We have festivals and parades celebrating everything from jazz to crawfish. The bars never close. Cocaine, cannabis, whores, loose women and pretty boys abound in the City That Care

Forgot. The Big Easy has always been a town where the citizens would rather play and party than sweat and slave. It would seem, at least to the man who made the comment about the Saints and the Cowboys, that this attitude of concupiscence is contagious and has infected the Saints as well.

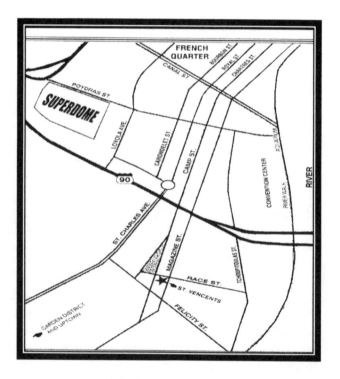

Louisiana Superdome Map

Perhaps there is another darker, more arcane reason for their abysmal performance. This has to do with the desecration of the dead. Allow me to explain further. The Louisiana Superdome was constructed on land that once held the Girod Street Cemetery. This was a Protestant necropolis that was founded in 1822 by Christ Church. As time progressed the Girod Street Cemetery fell into disrepair and ruin. In 1957 it was deconsecrated and demolished. Subsequently the Louisiana

Superdome was constructed on the site. The Superdome is the home field of the New Orleans Saints. Are the Saints the victims of the restless souls that once found peace in the lost cemetery? If you examine their record and all of their bad luck one is tempted to accept this notion as fact.

A Mystery

Metairie Cemetery is the premier cemetery in New Orleans. (Klein pp. 1-6 1996.) It was granted a charter in 1872 and the first interment took place in1873. Before that time it was a racetrack frequented by the aristocratic *Creoles of Nouvelle Orléans*. Those snobs hated the "Kaintucks" (corruption of the word Kentucky to which they referred to the Americans who assumed control of Louisiana in 1803). One individual toward whom they directed a special species of contempt was a wealthy American by the name of Charles T. Howard. He had the audacity to present himself at the racetrack one sweltering day in shirt sleeves sans the traditional wool frock coat. The Creoles were aghast at his arrogance and quickly expelled him admonishing him to never return (Fox, p. 30). He left with prophetic words, "One day I'll bury ya'll."

Was this a threat? What did he mean? After the Civil War the fortunes of many Creoles fell with slavery. The race track they once supported plummeted into debt. Howard purchased the grounds and turned it into, perhaps, the most fashionable cemetery in North America. The bones of many of the "gentlemen" who once rebuked him are now ensconced in his necropolis.

Now for the mystery. Many tombs have attendant mysteries. Rudolf Valentino's grave is visited by a lady in black. Edgar Allen Poe's resting spot also has an unknown pilgrim who on certain dates leaves flowers and liquor. Marilyn Monroe is visited on the anniversary of her death by an undetected mourner who also leaves gifts of remembrance.

Faithful Friend

Metairie Cemetery also plays host to a similar mysterious visitor. On Avenue H between the "old" and "new" sections of the graveyard is the Masich Tomb. When Arthur Masich died in 1893 his faithful dog followed his master's coffin to the crypt. The dog would not leave. Even though he was transported home time and again he would continue to return to his vigil. The faithful canine eventually died from a broken heart. The family requested that the beloved and loving companion be buried with his deceased master. Permission was refused — After all, he was *only* a dog! The family placed a statue in the dog's image to commemorate his devotion. To this very day flowers and ribbons are found adorning the statue always on Christmas and All Saints Day (1 November). This tradition has continued unabated for over a century. No one has ever witnessed the hand responsible for this loving tribute (Ibid; Gandolfo, p.104).

Time and Again

We are all locked in an eternal present based on memories of the past and anticipation of the future. St. Augustine remarked in his *Confessions*, "What is time?"

If no one asks him he knows. When asked he does not. The concept of Time defies an explicit definition.

We know phenomena displays four dimensions: length, breadth, height and time. Time is a fluid dimension in that the duration of a thing is continually expanding while the other dimensions (for all practical purposes) are static.

Humanity in the twentieth century has begun to understand the forces and materials that are responsible for the dynamics and sustenance of the universe. We are confronted with space/time, matter/energy, gravity/electromagnetism/the weak force/the strong force and a yet undiscovered, unrecognized force that I predict and describe in *Hermes and Christ: The Occult Unveiled* (p.173). Twenty-first century physics is concerned with a set of elegant formulae which will articulate all of these considerations into a unity — The Unified Field Theory. Once this task is complete we shall possess the grammar of creation.

Back to time. We all experience time. Philosophers and scientists not only experience time but examine it as well. We humans construct devices to measure the temporal dimension — movement of shadows, sand grains filling a vessel, hands moving across a calibrated face that tell us little about time as it actually exists. Such measuring devices are homogenous, i.e. seconds, hours, years differ only by the addition of one unit (second, hour, year). This time is a mathematical concept that is " . . . represented as an extended, homogenous medium composed of standard units" (Edwards, Volume I, pp. 287-288). It is a passive phenomenon.

Time exist apart from our synthetic measuring of it. Time also exist independently of our observation of it. If we did not exist time would continue to work its changes. Galaxies, stars, molecules and atoms would still experience change, evolution as they existed in time.

Henri Bergson (1859-1941) French evolutionary philosopher postulate a theory of time that is juxtaposed to the ideas about time as homogenous, mechanical and deterministic. Bergson saw time as heterogeneous, a concrete an indivisible process that is "immediately experienced as active and ongoing" (Ibid, p. 288).

It is this theory of time that I wish the reader to consider when reading about Popp's Fountain located in City Park. (For a historical description of City Park see *New Orleans Ghosts II*, pp. 20-23.)

I am a practicing occultist and ceremonial magician. As such I am always on the lookout for interesting places to do rituals with my church members. Popp's Fountain is superb for it is a large fountain surrounded by a perfect circle of Greek columns. It is also surrounded by oak trees (sacred to the ancient Celts and Druids.) It is a tremendous place for water rituals (when the Sun moves into the astrological signs of Cancer, Scorpio and Pisces). We have experienced manifestations of the "second order" utilizing this area for our endeavors. I believed that our experiences were limited to our practices until researching this present work. Kalila Katherina Smith's book (op. cit. pp. 56-5) cites the experience of certain individuals who realized peculiar temporal distortions at this site. She investigated the fountain using a variety of instruments which all showed significant aberrations: electromagnetic and thermal readings. She also indicated that photographic anomalies appeared at the location.

I must add that during my ritualistic practices at the fountain the one common experience that members of my church and I had were a disconcerting dislocation of our perception of time. Sometimes time dilated. Other times it contracted. The experiences were amazing, and I am happy to report that they were not unique to my group.

Circular Cascade

The Vanished Mansion

I n the year of Our Lord 1800 a remarkable man built a remarkable home on a forked road down river from the city. The man in question was one David Clark. He was remarkable for many reasons. Clark was of neither French or Spanish descent. An Irishman who came to represent Louisiana in the United States Congress after the colony became the eighteenth state in the Union in 1812.

He was a merchant who owned ships and plantations and properties. He had interests in cotton, oranges, sugar cane, indigo, timber, pelts, tobacco and the most lucrative of all slaves. Clark was immensely rich, powerful and influential. In New Orleans he was awarded the appellation, "the Irishman who became a Créole" (deLavigne, p. 305).

About his person it may be said that he was middle age, a bachelor and quite the playboy or *bon vivant* in the lingo of the time. He spoke French, Spanish, English and Gaelic and reinforced these linguistic attributes with the manners and refinements of the finest of Créole gentlemen. That coupled with a fortune of $30,000,000 dollars made him the grandest prize in the New World. Virtually every woman was at his feet — or in his bed! Daniel worked hard — and he played just as hard.

Being a clever, cunning man of business he early on realized the economic debilitating realities of marriage. A wife with endless demands on his purse. In-laws who anticipated — no, *expected* — gratuities. Let us not forget the demands of children — health care, education, entertainment, doweries for daughters and legal and illegal payments for sons. All of this he avoided by never courting marriage.

He invested some of his great wealth in the construction of his fabulous, rambling mansion. Fine marbles and sturdy granites combined with rare and exquisite woods were imported from around the globe on his ever traveling ships. Furniture and art from France, Italy, the Netherlands, Spain, Portugal and the British Isles decorated his walls and adorned his rooms. Rugs and carpets from Persia, India and the Empire of the Ottomans graced his polished, hardwood floors with passive elegance. His abode became his palace, his dome, his Xanadu. Life and living were great, perfect. The world was his oyster, and he suck his oyster dry of its delectable juices.

The Vanished Mansion
After all, it vanished!

One monumentally beautiful spring day our merchant-prince concluded some business on the docks. He decided to celebrate his continuing good fortune with some fine chocolates and a cocktail hour drenched with Absinthe. Walking from the wharf he passed by the lower Pontabla Building (See Klein, 1999, pp. 56-60) where his friend Jerome de Grange operated an upscale shop. As soon as Daniel entered the shop he was mesmerized by the exotic beauty of the proprietor's exotically beautiful spouse, Zuleme. She was of a sepia hue with cascades of bituminous, wavy locks falling to her wasp like waist. Her eyes appeared as coal. Her petite body perfectly housed the exaggerated curves of her breasts and derriere.

The calculating, cool merchant became possessed by the uncontrollable, volcanic fever of a love that was as esoteric and as hypnotic as the goddess who smiled before his bewildered and beguiled eyes. How he accomplished the task is not known, but within the hour he had convinced the shop keeper to become his agent. Before the sun had fallen twice Jerome was aboard one of Daniel's ships headed for Europe with cash, letters of introduction and credit.

When the fiery tentacles of dawn rendered the black of the night into radiant light Zuleme was in the bed and arms of the Irishman. He had never known such passion; such love; such fulfillment.

Clark investigated De Grange and learned that his marriage to the Romani was void since he was already married and never pursued a divorce (deLavigne, p. 309). Shortly thereafter Daniel and his consort sailed for Philadelphia where they were married in the embrace of the Roman Catholic Church.

As many a man and woman have testified marriage can alter drastically a fantastic, celestial relationship. Such was the case with Daniel and Zuleme. Upon their return the relationship began to denigrate by degrees. He began to see past the allure of her exotic beauty and ultra sexuality. Underneath these externals he perceived the internal reality of her uneducated coarseness; her violent temper; her basic poor taste in fashion and manners.

There was more. They engaged in fantastic sex every night; however, on the nights of the new and full moon when she thought he was asleep she would rise from their bed and gingerly descend the staircase to walk nude into the soft, moist night. He followed her one dark eve through the woods to a clearing where she met with a large group of Calo Gypsies. There in the hollow she would lead this disenfranchised tribe in obscure rituals of orgiastic dance dedicated to the appeasement of dark and forgot gods and goddesses. She was their High Priestess — their Queen! No wonder the Negro slaves steeped in Voodoo and the animism of the African continent lived in terror of her presence. Now he knew. She had bewitched him. She had stolen his heart, and God forbid, his soul as well.

The next morning after a fitful sleep she awakened him with the unearthly caress of her extraordinary fellatio. As his eyes opened she enlightened him about her pregnancy. But by whom, he pondered. Had his seed been planted in her dark, fertile field? Or was it a seed sown by Satan? His mind reeled with thoughts of eternal damnation. His power, prestige and privilege all paled before his realization of the ruin of his redemption. She must be expelled for the possibility of his salvation. Yet, he remained a man of honor and integrity. From his home she was driven, but not into the dark night of despair. Clark provided for her, and well indeed. She was ensconced in the French Quarter. Zuleme was given a luxurious suite with servants and the most accomplished physicians to attend her during her "confinement". Birth came. After her agony ended a new species of agony was applied to our passion filled gypsy.

Their daughter, Myra Clark Gaines was spirited away to Philadelphia to be educated and raised far from the Crescent City and her mother. Clark had business concerns and influence there. His money would hide the scandal of his sins.

Daniel underestimated Zuleme's resolve and love. She would not be paid off like a cheap whore. She was his wife. She bore him a child. She had rights, and privileges. Law and morality were on her side.

Under the cover of night she returned to claim her due. Madame Salaun, now the proprietress of the great house denied her access. Her screams and demands were relentless. As dawn revealed her pain to the light of the world Daniel Clark could endure no longer. Zuleme was granted entrance to *her* home only to suffer the introduction of an axe to her skull. The deed done, Daniel proceeded to dismember the corpse. He work manically cutting her into one hundred pieces. The fruits of his labor were distributed about the perimeters of his property. Vermin, heat and humidity would finish the task. Soon nothing remained. Daniel was safe. Daniel was free (Ibid, p. 311).

Daniel died a scant few years later in 1813. Declaring no heirs and leaving no will his properties and vast fortune fell prey to that greatest of all predators — lawyers. Business partners, creditors and yes, representatives of his daughter pursued relief until 1885 — seventy-two years ebbed before she was compensated for her efforts.

After Daniel's death his home was boarded and closed. Soon after the closure of his rambling mansion weird events began. One night a watchman noticed lights cascading from the deserted abode. Upon investigating he was met with a horrifying spectacle. After ascending to the second floor the man's eyes were assailed by a vision from hell. Within the great ballroom he observed what he estimated were a hundred dark, swarthy Gypsies engaged in obscene, unholy passions encircling a great fire dominated by a lithe, beautiful, sepia vixen. He reached for his sidearm and cutlass. The guard barked his authority to the assemblage. Before the echo of his voice faded the Gypsy Queen, her entourage and the great fire vanished. The distraught sentinel reported the orgy to his superiors. When a group of armed men investigated they were amazed to find the room of the alleged debacle vanished.

Throughout the years reports of mysterious lights continued until, eventually, the entire mansion was no more. Zuleme claimed her home, her privilege, her right. She and her hundred pieces of flesh maintained their reclamation until Daniel Clark's home was no more.

Josephine

One of the avenues of research I followed in writing *New Orleans Ghosts III* was experiencing some of the many ghost tours that have come into existence since I first opened the field to commercial exploitation with *New Orleans Ghosts*, 1993. May 2003 I met with a group in the Garden District (that area of the city settled by the "Americans" shortly after the Louisiana Purchase of 1803 and roughly bounded by avenues Jackson, St. Charles and Louisiana and Magazine Street).

We were soon standing at the majestic 21,000 square foot Buckner House built in 1856. As of this date (2004), it is the largest private residence in the Garden District. I might also remark that, in my opinion, it is one of the most beautiful and imposing homes that I have ever seen in an urban location.

The day of our tour was a beautiful spring day. Our guide was a personable, animated young man named Kevin. He was a representative of Haunted History Tours owned by Sidney Smith, whose wife also wrote a book about the ghosts of New Orleans, *Journey into Darkness*. I mention this because before the publication of *New Orleans Ghosts*, there existed only one book written exclusively about the ghosts of the Crescent City and that was Jeanne deLavigne's 1946 work *Ghost Stores of Old New Orleans*. Subsequent to my work, no fewer than one dozen books have been published dealing with the *spectres* of the "Big Easy" making the ghosts of New Orleans the most written about in the United States. Kalia Smith's book is noteworthy in that it is well researched and written and she lists my work in her bibliography. Enough on that topic.

Our guide related the following story to our group. Before the Civil War, the Buckner's owned a slave by the name of Josephine. Even though she was held in bondage, she was devoted to "her" family. She kept their palatial home in immaculate condition. New Orleans was one of the most unhealthy cities in North America because its climate was hot and humid and the perfect breeding ground for bacteria and disease carrying vermin. Its status as a world class sea port contributed to this problem by not only importing agricultural and industrial products but alien pathogens as well. Josephine combated this problem by insisting that the servants under her supervision maintained the highest standards of cleanliness and hygiene. It was also rumored that she practiced Voo-Doo to further discourage the evil spirits of disease and death. The Buckners remained surprisingly healthy for the time and their good health was due in no small way to the efforts of their faithful housekeeper.

The Civil War came and with it the ruination of the South. Slavery ended. No longer was the Negro held in the chains of bondage. Josephine was now free; however, she did not leave the Buckners. She elected to stay and continue to serve and love them until her death sometime in the early twentieth century. Even death could not erase her devotion. Until this very day evidence of her concern continues. Residents of the home report that dirty dishes are cleaned by an unseen hand. Floors are mopped and waxed defying any rational explanation. Finally, vermin are inexplicably rare considering the huge population of rats and roaches which have ruled the area from time immemorial. Perhaps the poets are right — Love does conquer Death!

The Tragic Triangle

In 1870 John Pelham brought his Mobile born wife Caroline Andrews to New Orleans to share in his life, in his dreams, in his love. She was a petite girl with flowing, thick, chestnut hair and a porcelain complexion. John was a maturing man past thirty. Caroline was but twenty-two yet appeared even younger with her shy ways and doll-like countenance.

John loved her as the flowers love the sun and rain. He worked hard to provide for her. He gave her a comfortable home on a corner lot with a beautiful garden filled with herbs and fragrant flowers. The house was cool during the long, baking summers and cozy during the short, damp winters. The couple were in love and happy. On the surface everything appeared utopian, but fair Caroline had a dark secret. It was one Joseph Curtis.

Curtis was a charmer. Tall. Educated. Well dressed. He had married a wealthy woman who loved him insanely. While still in her teens Caroline had fallen for the married cad Curtis and carried on an extensive, exquisite, forbidden affair. Realizing the error of her ways and the futility of such a dalliance Caroline opted for responsibility and a future with Pelham. Victorian morality being what it was she never informed her husband of Curtis or the affair.

Shortly after their arrival in the city when John had left for his daily toil the doorbell rang. Caroline knew who it was. She opened the door and there stood a beaming Joe (deLavigne, p. 260).

"Well, I kept my word — here I am."

"Yes." Breathlessly she stammered, "And I'm so frightened, Joe! Suppose someone saw you and told John!" (Ibid).

Her words meant nothing to him. Joe seized her in his arms and their passion was soon renewed. Only this time their loving embraces were more intense, more forbidden. This time they were both married, and this added more fuel to their furnace founded on sex and sin.

The weeks that followed were both a dream and a nightmare. While the sun burned its signature in the sweltering New Orleans days she and Joe enjoyed the passions reserved for the damned. At night when the moon reigned she endured the occasional mechanistic clutches of her simple, trusting spouse. Her emotions tore at the fabric of her sanity. She felt love and repulsion, satisfaction and guilt, elation and despair and, oh, yes, she felt rage and hatred. Caroline felt rage for John. She hated Joe for not leaving his wealthy wife and consummating their love with legitimacy, with marriage. And, most certainly she hated Joe for the fruit of fear that their illicit love bore.

Caroline found her life confused and confusing, but the worst was yet to come. She was pregnant! When she told John he was beside himself with joy. Now they would be a "real" family with a child with whom they could share their love. John showered her with kisses and the most tender, passionate love she had ever experienced with him. Such joy, such love only added to her guilt and perplexity. Her emotions, her life, her very being were lost beyond any semblance of control.

When she informed Joe of her condition he replied with a cynical laugh and sardonic words.

"It is mine. It is mine, of course, although John will get the credit for it. We'll make a bargain: if it's a boy, it's mine; if it's a girl, it's John's (Ibid, p. 262).

For several months nothing changed except her slim body. She grew with child which only seemed to increase the ardor of her two men. The pregnancy, the never ceasing sex and her guilt and anxiety took their tool. Again events changed. One afternoon Joe informed Caroline that he must leave for a while. How long he did not know, but he would return one day. With these words slamming against the canyons and valleys of her mind he took his leave.

Time ebbed. The child was born. It was a boy. John was ecstatic. Caroline fretted. Would her son, named Louis, grow to resemble Joe with his dark good looks and glib charming way, or would he be dull and average like John?

The years formed Louis into the image of Joe. John seemed not to notice. His only interest was in his family not the child's appearance. Caroline settled into her life as wife and mother, yet Joe always haunted her tortured mind. Would he return? If so, when? She could not endure the passion, the guilt, the shame and fear that were her bedfellows those several years previous.

One morning Joe left for work as was his custom. It was a brilliant, sunny summer's day. Louis was enjoying his vacation in the backyard whittling a soft piece of pine wood. Caroline was engaged in her domestic duties. The doorbell shattered her harmony. She knew it was Joe!

She opened the door and there he stood. Still handsome and urbane but he appeared dissipated. His hair was now snow white.

"Still playing at housekeeping. I hear the child was a boy. Let me see him, Caroline" (Ibid, 263).

"No, no, no, no. I can't! My life would be at an end — everything would be at an end! How can you come back like this, to blot out my future and spoil my boy's life?"

She screamed. She cried. The sounds of her distress drew Louis into their house. Joe turned laughing madly. When his eyes fell upon the boy he bellowed, "So, here is my boy, I should know him in a thousand....And did you name him after me, as was proper?" (Ibid)

After an uneventful day's work John Pelham returned to an empty house. Caroline and Louis were nowhere to be found. He searched the house and found nothing out of place. The breakfast dishes were still in the sink. No clothes nor effects had been taken. Caroline's sunbonnet was still on the peg as was Louis' cap. John replayed the events of the morning. No matter how he examined his memories he could surface no clue to explain the disappearance of his family. He kept hoping, praying for their return, for a return of normalcy. Dawn replaced the night — still no word, no sign. John began his inquiries. The neighbors, the police, her family in Mobile all resulted in vain efforts.

The days dragged onward. John became almost zombie-like — a walking corpse with no glimmer of release. The once bountiful garden became overgrown with weeds and vines. One dismal night the neighborhood was aroused with maniacal shrieks. John Pelham was running helter skelter down the darkened streets gripped by insanity and pursued by fear. A neighbor Henry Cardinal, attempted to comfort him.

"It's them. It's her and it's him — Caroline and the boy! I was sitting there in front of the fireplace, and she walked right out of it! The fire spluttered and went out, and then she came standing in front of me! And then he came — Louis just as he used to be!"

"You mean the ghosts of them?" inquired Mrs. Cardinal with fright drapped words (Ibid, 264).

"Yes, the ghosts of them! She leered and snarled at me like a she-wolf, her teeth long and yellow and her eyes like balls of fire! I thought she was going to claw me — and the boy was to the right of her. It was dreadful...but I've got to go back. It's my house and she can't drive me out of it!" (Ibid).

As the years passed the hauntings continued to molest poor John's sanity. He would question the angry, hateful specters in his mind. Why would Caroline come back to haunt him with such malevolence? She loved him. They were a happy family. Why? Why? Why?

The neighbors also speculated. Their speculations were not concerned so much with the hauntings, as with the whys and wherefores of the little family's disappearance. There was probably another man involved. Who was he though? Did Pelham discover the indiscretion, and in a fit of jealous insanity kill and dispose of the participants and his son who witnessed the carnage? Were these vengeful ghosts real or only projections of John Pelham's deranged senses? Questions, unanswered questions abounded.

Brokenhearted John Pelham finally died. The ghosts didn't. The house passed through a succession of owners. Some remained a few days. None stayed more than three weeks. Each beleaguered inhabitant of the once charming cottage reported the same dreadful apparitions — a she-wolf daemon and her spawn from hell emanating from the fireplace with fierce fury and rage projecting them toward the petrified occupants.

One courageous man stood his ground with bravery that was rewarded with a vicious mauling (Ibid, p. 266).

The house remained unoccupied for years. Rabbits, rats and bats ruled. The cottage was shunned. Finally, a group of Germans elected to buy the property, renovate it, and transform it into a school for German-Americans where English and German would be taught. They knew the history of the house; however, they reasoned that the building would be used as a school and not a continually inhabited home, and that since the hauntings seemed to occur only at night they should be safe from any undue happenings. They were in error. Every morning at 10:00 o'clock a harpie flew from the fireplace to reek havoc on the senses and minds of the students and their teachers.

Once again the place fell into abandonment and ruin. So it remained as the years marched onward. The fragrant Magnolia tree that once stood majestically in the front garden was struck by lightening and turned into a skeletal guardian of the macabre secrets within the walls of the rotting structure.

The Spanish-American War came and went, and with that war of American colonial expansion came a resolution to our story, and with it the mystery that animated it. A small, dark, Hispanic man by the name of Miguel Alvarez arrived in New Orleans at the turn of the last century. He was in possession of a large sum of money, a wedding ring and a story filled with horror and angst. While in Cuba Alvarez was imprisoned for a political offense. While so ensconced he shared a cell with one Joseph Curtis. Curtis died during his period of incarceration, but before he departed on the wings of death he bequeath to Miguel a large sum of money, a wedding ring belonging to Caroline Andrew Pelham and the following confession which this author quotes in its entirety from the pages of Jeanne deLavigne's tome (see Bibliography).

"'He confessed to a foul crime," the Spaniard told the man who then owned the haunted house. "It seems he had been this Mrs. Pelham's lover, and he believed himself to be the father of her son. The day he visited her he saw the son for the first time, and it sent him into a frenzy of hatred for the man she had married.

"Suddenly he wanted to marry her himself. His own unloved wife had died, and he was free. He urged Mrs. Pelham to flee with him, telling her that her own husband was maintaining a mistress. But she cut his words short, pushing him away from her and refusing his propositions and his arguments.

"Filled with mad fury against her husband and remembering the years of fear and misery occasioned by her lover, she was like a maniac. He seized her by the throat and bent her backward over his knees until he heard her spine snap. Then, half-insane himself, and with the boy fighting him off, he pulled back her head and rammed a broomstick down her throat and into her body with one frightful thrust. Laughing, he grasped the boy, flung him over the newel post and broke his back. He said it seemed as though a tide of blood were rushing at him, smothering him and drowning him in its crimson horror.

"Still loving her as he did, he felt no remorse for what he had done. It was as though the Devil drove him. The dead woman and her boy now seemed impersonal — objects of which he must dispose, but which really did not concern him and of which he had no understanding.

"He pried up one of the hearthstones and found a convenient cavity beneath it. Digging down into the soft earth, he buried the two bodies, covering them well.

"Then he cleaned up every trace of the deed, waited until dusk, and left the house and the city. I wish now to buy the place with the money he gave me. I shall set in it in order and occupy it with my family."

The transaction was completed in a few days. The first thing Alvarez did was to have workmen remove the great hearthstone and dig under it. There they found the bones of a woman and a boy, wrapped in an old carpet. The skeletons were removed and buried beside John Pelham.

From that time on, no ghosts ever appeared in the little house where Caroline had known love and pain and terror and remorse and death (Ibid, 267-268).

My Ghost

As of this date (10 June 2004) I have been a published, professional author specializing in occult/paranormal literature for over seventeen years. In that period I have published the immensely successful and influential *New Orleans Ghosts* series. I have investigated and researched almost seventy ghost stories centered around New Orleans.

I have learned that what people interpret as encounters with ghosts are extremely common. How valid these experiences are is open to speculation and analysis based on in-depth empirical investigations. I have not had the time nor inclination to investigate these myriad reports outside of those that I have documented and researched in my sundry published works.

While creating this present book I realized that Jean deLavigne and I are the foundation upon which all subsequent efforts have been constructed. As I stated earlier these subsequent works provided me with stories of which I was unacquainted or only found scant biographical material. These later works filled in those gaps and have allowed me to flesh out my third and final contribution to revenant folklore concerning my city's unrested souls. As I wrote I found fewer and fewer good, entertaining tales. Then, suddenly, I reflected on all of those people I've met at book signings, lectures, parties and bars who upon learning of my efforts confided paranormal stories to me. I realized that apart from my documented intercourse with those who dwell beyond (Klein, 1996, pp. 1-6, pp. 13-22; Klein, 2000, pp. 46-51) I have been in a seventeen year relationship with a continuing and continual paranormal theater of events. I shall now explain and examine this assertion.

In 1987 I began residence in a two story, Edwardian home in the uptown, university section of New Orleans. The house was constructed in 1906 and was the residence of one Podine Schoenberger. She was a lady of note. Ms. Schoenberger (she never married) was a journalist and newspaper reporter who worked for the now defunct *Shates-Item*. Upon her death the estate passed to several heirs who rented the property to young professionals until my family purchased it in 1987.

The house and out buildings (carport and small servants' quarters) required a great deal of work since the heirs simply rented the property and were not too keen about investing in renovations or repairs. After my family purchased the home my father, friends, relatives and I began the long, slow, steady process of an "architectural" make over.

During one period of such work I was cleaning out the underneath of the house (it rests on about two dozen brick pilings which elevate the house about three feet from the ground). There were bottles, bricks, discarded boards, trash, nothing of undue interest or concern. After a cursory policing I took a garden rake with me to level the ground. I found a silver crucifix. In the course of about two hours I found three medals (all silver) depicting varying Catholic saints. I kept them.

Having always been interested in religion, the occult, etc., etc., I theorized that because of the Catholic/Voodoo heritage of the Big Easy these icons were in some fashion related to this pedigree. I was amused.

As soon as we moved in I began to notice bizarre events transpiring within our new home's walls. First, at dawn or dusk there seemed to be some areas in certain rooms that appeared darker than the rest. A second factor was that the house was plagued by continual dust and dirt. The air conditioner filters became useless after a week or so. My experience in uptown New Orleans is that they are usually good for about six weeks. The floors are always dirty, leaving the soles of one's feet black despite weekly moppings with detergent. Finally, the most frustrating and devastating reality is the continual disappearance of various elements of property.

The disappearances require an in-depth description and analysis. Everyone misplaces objects, papers, money, but nothing to the strange extent that transpires at our Audubon Street address. The litany of vanishings and usual returns is astronomical. I shall only describe the more dramatic and memorable of them.

My mother was given a gold wristwatch by my father. She cherished it; only wearing it on special occasions. After we had been in residence in the house for about one year my mother and father were celebrating their wedding anniversary. She elected to wear her expensive, gold watch that evening. Upon opening her jewelry box she discovered it was gone. To this day it has not surfaced.

I am a bibliophile who numbers among my rare books a first English translation edition of Mao-tse-Tung's *Red Book*, Peking, 1966. I keep this book with about 400 other collector oriented works in a special bookcase. Over the past 17 years this book has vanished and reappeared in other parts of the house on four separate occasions.

I own two Egyptian, brass candle holders. One of the set has disappeared twice. As of this writing it is still missing. Same with an antique derringer that has vanished and then materialized on six separate occasions.

I shall have papers on my desk. I put them in a particular place depending what they are: bills, box A, letters, box B, phone numbers, box C, and so on. Usually in a day or so it reappears in the same box that I had searched methodically the previous evening.

These occurrences are so common and so frustrating that my mother told one of her friends about this phenomenon. Her friend is a Roman Catholic. Her friend informed her of the Catholic belief that if an object is lost one should promise St. Antony of Padua a monetary token for its return (I discuss St. Antony in *New Orleans Ghosts II*, pp. 68-69.) I am not a Catholic. I am not a Christian. Not withstanding, and grasping at straws I began the practice. Let me say that if something was not where it should be I thought it was misplaced, not vanished and would initiate a search. It usually surfaced; however, some things did not fit the criterium of simply being misplaced. Prime example: one week ago I presented my mother with some important documents that required her signature. She signed them. I placed them in an envelope on the coffee table and retired for the night. The next morning I decided to walk Wolfen, my German Shepherd Dog, and mail the papers. They were gone! I searched the living room. My mother searched the living room. My son searched the living room. The papers could not be found. This meant another visit to my attorney, and another fee! My mother did the St. Anthony pledge. She went to the living room to read a magazine while waiting for a friend to pick her up for lunch. The envelope and papers were on top of the magazine for which she reached.

The final thread in this carpet of malicious absurdity happened the very day I am writing this chapter. I am a numismatist — I collect coins. 20 April I purchased an 1854 United States 1/4 dollar. I brought it home. In lieu of depositing it in one of my safe-deposit boxes I placed it in a desk drawer as is my custom. The next morning it was gone. I searched the drawer; the desk; my office; my home; my clothes; my cars; my memorabilia. It was gone! I did the St. Antony thing — to no avail. Time passed. I awoke today. I went into my computer lab to check my faxes and e-mail. The coin was in a plastic container that serves as a receptacle for paperclips, stamps, rubber bands, et al. I asked my mother, my son, my business partner Keith Nicholson about the coin. They all professed ignorance.

I am tired of this abuse. I am a ceremonial magician — a *Magus Adeptus*. Part of my writing this chapter is to initiate an exorcism against this never-ending bullshit. Enough is enough. The Buddhists initiate their magickal prayer requests through Prayer Wheels. These are hand held devices that can be rotated thousands of times in an hour to throw a massive quantitative request to the Gods. My Prayer Wheel is this book which shall be printed tens of thousands of times in my ebbing lifetime.

I begin by saying I banish thee poltergeist — pesky spirit. I indict you using the most powerful of all spells, incantations and rebuttals against thee. Now, my nemesis face the power of Solomon.

BOOK ONE.

CHAPTER IX.

Of The Experiment Concerning Things Stolen, and How It Should Be Performed.

My beloved Son, if thou findest any Theft, thou shalt do as is hereinafter ordained, and with the help of God thou shalt find that which hath been taken away.

If the hours and days be not otherwise ordained in this operation, thou must refer to what hath already been said. But before commencing any operation whatsoever for the recovery of things stolen, after having made all necessary preparations, thou shalt say the following Oration:—

THE ORATION

Ateh Adonai Elohim Asher Ha-Shamain Ve-Ha-Artez, &c.

Thou, O Lord, Who hast made both Heaven and Earth, and hast measured them in the hollow of Thy hand; Thou Who art seated upon the Kerubim and the Seraphim, in the highest places, whereunto human understanding cannot penetrate; Thou Who hast created all things by Thine agency, in Whose Presence are the Living Creatures, of which four are marvelously volatile, which have six wings, and who incessantly cry aloud: "QADOSCH, QADOSCH, QADOSCH, ADONAI ELOHIM TZABAOTH, Heaven and Earth are full of Thy Glory;" O Lord God, Thou Who hast expelled Adam from the Terrestrial Paradise, and Who hast placed the Kerubim to guard the Tree of Life, Thou art the Lord Who alone doest wonders; show forth I pray Thee Thy Great Mercy, by the Holy City of Jerusalem, by Thy wonderful Name of four letters which are *YOD, HE, VAU, HE*, and by Thy Holy and Admirable Name, give unto me the power and virtue to enable me to accomplish this experiment, and to come unto the desired end of this operation; through Thee Who art Life, and unto Whom Life belongeth unto the eternal ages. Amen.

After this perfume and cense the place by burning *Temple Incense*. This aforesaid place should be pure, clean, safe from interruption or disturbance, and proper to the work, as we shall heretofore show. Then sprinkle the aforesaid place with consecrated Water, as is laid down in the *Chapter concerning Circles.*

The Operation being in such wise prepared, thou shalt rehearse the Conjuration necessary for this experiment, at the end of which Thou shalt say as follows:—

O Almighty Father and Lord, Who regardest the Heavens, the Earth, and the Abyss, mercifully grant unto me by Thy Holy Name written with four letters, *YOD, HE, VAU, HE,* that by this exorcism I may obtain virtue, Thou Who art *IAH, IAH, IAH,* grant that Thy power the Spirits may discover that which we require and which we hope to find, and may they show and declare unto us the persons who have committed the theft, and where they are to be found.

I conjure ye over this burning Temple Incense, anew, ye Spirits above named, by all the aforesaid Names, through which all things created tremble, that ye show openly unto me (or unto this child here present with us[1]) those tings which we seek.

These things being accomplished they will make thee to see plainly that which thou seekest. Take note that the Exorcist, or Master of the Arts, should be such as is ordained in the Chapter concerning the Exorcist and his Companions; and if in this experience it should be necessary to write down character or Names, thou shalt do that which it is necessary to observe regarding the pen, ink, and paper, as is duly prescribed in the chapters concerning them.

For if thou dost not regard these thins, thou wilt neither accomplish that which thou desirest, nor arrive at thy desired end.

---

[1]A child employed as a clairvoyant in the operation; as is still the custom in some places in the East.

HOW TO KNOW WHO HAS COMMITTED A THEFT

Take a Sieve,[2] after burning one-half teaspoonful of *Temple Incense*, and suspend it by a piece of cord wherewith a man has been hung, which should be fastened round the circumference of the rim. Within the rim write with blood in the four divisions thereof the characters given in Figure 4. After this take a basin of brass perfectly clean which thou shalt fill with water from a fountain, and having pronounced these words: *DIES MIES YES-CHET BENE DONE FET DONNIMA METEMAUZ*, make the sieve spin round with thy left hand, and at the same time turn with thy right hand the water in the basin in a contrary direction, by stirring it with a twig of green laurel. When the water becometh still and the sieve no longer whirls, gaze fixedly into the water, and thou shalt see th form of him who hath committed the theft; and in order that thou mayest the more easily recognize him, thou shalt mark him in some part of his face with the Magical Sword of Art; for that sign which thou shalt have cut therewith in the water, shall be really found thereafter upon his own person.

THE MANNER OF CAUSING THE SIEVE TO TURN, THAT THOU MAYEST KNOW WHO HAS COMMITTED THE THEFT

Take a Sieve and stick into the outside of the rim the open points of a pair of scissors, and having rested the rings of the said opened scissors on the thumb-nails of two persons, let one of them say the following Prayer:—

---

[2]sieve >noun a utensil consisting of a wire or plastic mesh held in a frame, used for straining solids from liquids or separating coarser from finer particles.

PRAYER

DIES MIES YES-CHET BENE DONE FET DONNIMA METEMAUZ; O Lord, Who liberatedest the holy Susanna from a false accusation of crime; O Lord, Who liberatedest the holy Thekla; O Lord, Who rescuedest the holy Daniel from the den of lions, and the Three Children from the burning fiery furnace, free the innocent and reveal the guilty.

After this let him or her pronounce aloud the names and surnames of all the persons living in the house where theft hast been committed, who may be suspected of having stolen the things in question, saying:—

"By Saint Peter and Saint Paul, such a person hath not done this thing."

And let the other reply:—

"By Saint Peter and Saint Paul, he (or she) hath not done it."

Let this be repeated thrice for each person named and suspected, and it is certain that on naming the person who hath committed the theft or done the crime, the sieve will turn of itself without its being able to stop it, and by this thou shalt know the evil doer (DeLaurence, *The Greater Key of Solomon*, pp. 42-44).

Knox Om Pax
So Mote It Be

Fan Mail

Being a popular author is nothing but pluses. I enjoy book signings at fairs, festivals, lectures, libraries, stores and shops. I have appeared on approximately a dozen television programs and probably three times that many radio shows. On occasion people recognize me and engage me in conversations about my books, my works, my thoughts. I have an identity. I'm an author. I have relative immortality. My books and therefore my ideas will stretch across the chasm of time far beyond my death.

Beside these realities the most sincere form of appreciation comes wrapped in an envelop–the "fan letter." I've received praise, propositions, pronouncements, judgements, scorn, critiques and just about everything else one can imagine.

I have decided to devote a chapter to several of these letters in order to reveal something of the appreciation (positive and negative) that I have had from my devoted readers. I believe it will be fun, and informative and also accomplish something for me. Writers write for a variety of reasons; however, they all share a common thread in the fabric of their creativity. All writers feel a sense of loneliness, alienation that they wish to exorcise. This exorcism takes the form of the written word. Each one of us, either covertly or overly, wishes a relationship with the "other." Our works open the door for this situation. The letters elicited by my works which I share with you communicate something about myself that I consider important. When you read these letters and my commentary realize that they are representative of what I feel is of importance in regard to what I have revealed of myself through the creative medium of my writing and the external responses they have engendered. With this in mind read and begin to understand this author. Letter #1 is what ghost hunters appreciate. It contains much data: a specific location (address), time (date), names and a detailed narrative.

Lynn Brown   *4900 E. 5th St., Apt 318, Tucson, AZ 85711*
          (502) 584-8469
          Tdove26@yahoo.com

September 9, 2000

Dear Mr. Klein,
     I am a former resident of New Orleans and a current fan of your work. I have both your books New Orleans Ghosts I and II, and I thought that as a researcher of ghost stories, specifically in New Orleans, you might be able to help me with a mystery. At the very least this story should give you a head start on research for a third book.
     As I have mentioned I was a resident of New Orleans for some time. I attended UNO for 2 years and lived in the city for a year or so after that. I had an apartment in the French Quarter on Chartres. 210 Chartres, Apt 3E to be exact. My roommates and I are convinced that the place was haunted and I was wondering if perhaps you'd heard anything.
     Apartment 3E was a two bedroom apartment over a Civil War store. I don't think we were the only apartments in the building, however I do think we were the only one that was haunted. Apparently the man who lived there before us (this would be in '98) "went crazy." This was mentioned to me after I'd already moved in, by one of the people that worked with my landlord, when I mentioned that I suspected that the place was haunted.
     The first bedroom, where I slept was covered with strange drawings and random phrases carved into the walls and the closet. The landlord had apparently tried to paint over the drawings, but it hadn't worked very well, although none of us remember seeing the paintings before we moved in. I don't remember most of the words that were written into the walls, however I do remember something to the effect of "she is me"

or "I am her," something like that. Although it is possible that I'm confusing the phrase with something else entirely.

The second bedroom in our apartment was always freezing cold. It also gave off a feeling of fear and confusion if you walked into it. Needless to say none of us wanted to sleep in there so the door [was] left closed. Not that it stayed that way.

The bathroom was right next to this room and had an inner and an outer door. If you closed the outer door (closest to the second bedroom door) you couldn't get it open again. It was as if someone were holding the door closed from the other side, and the only time you could get it open was if another person began to walk up the stairs. Then it would fly open, as if the pressure had been suddenly removed.

The apartment had a small spiral staircase leading into the livingroom and kitchen. On several occasions while sitting alone in the livingroom I saw what seemed to be the lower half of someone's body standing on the stairs. If you looked directly at the legs however it would move upward and disappear. On one such occasion my cat was walking up these stairs and suddenly flew off the side, as if kicked. At some point I got really irritated with the thing and told it to leave me alone, after that I didn't see the feet so much anymore. I'm not quite sure if my roommates saw anything after that point.

What else? There was the "monster food" incident. On several different occasions, while cooking, each of us saw the words "monster food" appear in red on the wall just behind the stove. None of us are sure if the writing was always there and just appeared because of the steam or what. However I'm pretty sure each of us only saw it once, it did not appear every time we were cooking.

There were four of us living in this apartment at the time, only one of the four being male. Our friend Cameron grew increasingly agitated and violent during the time that we lived there, where before he'd always been a very calm introspective kind of guy. He would pick fights constantly for no reason, fly into rages, and became very physical. I'm not sure if this is because of the haunting (we've nicknamed the ghost "monster food"), but I thought it was very interesting when you consider that the person who lived there before us was also a man, and also apparently had the same reaction to living there. Recently I ran into Cameron again and he has almost no recollection of the six months that we lived in this apartment, something else that I found rather odd.

If you've heard anything about this apartment being haunted or if you decide to look into it further please let me know. I am very interested in learning more about what went on in this apartment, even if it doesn't turn out to be haunted. I can be reached at the address or e-mail above.

Sincerely,

Lynn Brown

The second communication is complimentary and also offers the chance of a meeting with a woman who appreciates my art.

THE INTL. SOCIETY FOR THE STUDY OF GHOSTS AND APPARITIONS

Dear Victor:

I recently returned from New Orleans where my purpose was to photograph La Maison LaLaurie and see if I could pick up any vibes–(and to dine, of course).

I have both your ghost books . . . 1 & 2 . . . and find them of great help and interest.

As you can see by the enclosed flyer, I am very much into the genre myself. And what fun to live in a house haunted by Eleanor R.

I may be back in NOLA next March (or so) for a Tennessee Williams con. Perhaps we could get together for a little chat then. Or whenever . . .

Best Regards,

Jeanne Keyes Youngson

29 Washington Square West, NYC, NY 10011

Epistle three is disturbing, strange, bizarre and exactly the type of correspondence I relish. This letter and the person who wrote it interests me.

William A. Kingman
6521 Kawanee Avenue
Metairie, LA 70003

Victor C. Klein
P.O. Box 9028
Metairie, LA 70005-9028

Dear Mr. Klein,

I read your most recent book "New Orleans Ghosts II" with both pleasure and a bit of disdain. In particular the part entitled "The Phantom of the Ax". Unfortunately you fall into the same trap as many others who have written about the "Ax Man of New Orleans," lack of research. Most people, you included, quote Robert Tallant's book, "Ready to Hang." Most people usually go on further to quote "Gumbo Ya-Ya." It is interesting that, you in particular make great pains to point out your educational background, and your bibliography. Unfortunately you have decided to base your research on a previously published book without making sure that the facts contained in the previously published book are even accurate. Based on that, I would give your writing an "A", but your research an "F".

On page 93 paragraph three, you state, "During this time, five individuals, all Italian grocers and their wives, had fallen victim to an identical, brutal attack. The first victim was a man named Cruti, then Mr. And Mrs. Rosetti, and finally Mr. And Mrs. Tony Sciambra. You are correct in the fact that all these persons were victims, unfortunately Mr. And Mrs. Sciambra were victims of gun shot wounds. In fact, the coroner's report, which is available at the New Orleans Public Library if you so decide to research, says "**The Jurors**, whose names are hereunto subscribed, having been duly sworn and charged diligently inquire, on behalf of the State of Louisiana, how, when, and after what matter the said **Anthony J. Sciambra** came to **his** death, and upon their oaths do say — that after viewing an autopsy of said body do declare the death was the result of **Perforating gun shot wound of body internal hemorrage.**" [sic] The actual homicide reports, which surprisingly are also available at the New Orleans Public Library, say "Corporal Duffy entered into the residence walking to the bedroom found the nude body of Sciambra, lifeless, with three pistol shots in the back, once in the right side of the body and once in the right arm, and he lay on the floor a few feet away from the bed. Stretched across the bed was his wife who was suffering with a pistol wound to the left hip." (I have enclosed a copy of the Coroner's report for your edification.)[3]

On page 99 you say "At least the axman had a sense of fair play. His appreciation of jazz and absurdity prompted New Orleanians to initiate axman parties and to even publish a musical tribute to the daemon titled, The Mysterious Axmans's Jazz." The Times-Picayune on March 20, 1919, published an article entitled "DAVILLA COMPOSES "THE AXMAN'S JAZZ", but yet you seem to get that wrong also.

Page 101 "Addendum: A fact (possibly salient; possibly coincidental) was brought to the attention of the NOPD. The LAPD reported than an Orleanian, one Joseph Mumpre, had been gunned down by a woman in black and heavily veiled. (Talent, 1952, p. 184)." Tallant's book on page 214 (184?) Says, "On December 2, 1920, an Orleanian named Joseph Mumfre was walking down a Los Angeles business street in the early afternoon. A "woman in black and heavily veiled" stepped from the doorway of a sunny sidewalk and the woman stood over him, making no attempt to escape or even to move." Where did you come up with Mumpre?

I went to LA several years ago, and while I was there I went to the local library and checked out the newspapers of the era. A murder back then would be news. Nothing. I then went to the LA county records, nothing, no Joseph Mumfre/Mumpre killed in LA during that period. I wrote to the State of California for a copy of Mr. Mumfre's death certificate (enclosed). According to the state of California, there was no Joseph Mumfre who died in the state of California from 1915 to 2000.

---

[3]see Appendix

I have been researching this topic for years and it never ceases to amaze me that because it was written before, in particular, Tallant, it is now accepted as the truth. I have researched the local newspapers, libraries, etc for information on the "Ax Man", and have copies of several hundred stories, but no published author, has seemed to get it right. Nice try, but no cigar.

I wish you would contact me, you can reach me at the above address or my e-mail address is kingma3@attglobal.net.

The final letter is a critique which, as a scientist, I welcome. Also included with this letter was original documentation which is presented in Appendix E.

Because these letters were addressed to me they are my personal property and I may do with them as I wish. For bibliographic integrity I publish them verbatim–names, addresses, e-mails, phone numbers, etc. The expectation of privacy is null and void in such instances.

Epilogue

With *New Orleans Ghosts III* I concluded the series on my paranormal investigation of the city I love — New Orleans. My efforts have rewarded me in ways I could never express. I have published a total of eighteen nonfiction works as of this writing 15 May 2004. Apart from what my *New Orleans Ghost* series have done for the tourism industry in New Orleans the collection has also stimulated serious interest and research in the specific area of local paranormal activities and general interest in Thanatology and the occult. My works have impacted positively the existing body of recorded knowledge and in their own modest way added a tributary to the great river of history. *The Louisiana Collection* at Tulane University houses my personal papers, notes, letters and ephemera for the interest of present and future researchers, scholars, academics and occultists. For their interest in and preservation of this material I wish to express my eternal gratitude to Ken Owen, M.L.S. and Wilbur Meneray, Ph.D. As a history undergrad minor and a Master of Library Science (M.L.S.) Professional I desire to underscore my appreciations and love for libraries. These institutions are at the foundation of every civilization. I am honored to have my efforts represented and maintained in their collections.

I conceptualize my books as my children — my gifts to posterity. They shall outlive me and do more honor for my name that I did in my life and through my actions. I am an only child. Both of my parents worked at outside professions throughout most of my life. As such I was a lonely lad who has carried that loneliness with me to this very moment. When a boy I arrested that loneliness through books. Books were my first friends, first confidants, my first lovers. Books were magic and magical for me. They were my flying carpet, my looking glass, my Nautalis, my vehicle of escape and adventure. Some kids want to grow up to be firemen or ballerinas or cowboys or pimps. Not me, baby! I wanted to become a writer. I did it. Alright, enough ego trash.

I leave my readers with a final thought. Alfred North Whitehead remarked in his *Principia* (written in conjunction with Bernard Russell) that no question, framed properly, cannot be answered. The great question that has plagued and befuddled humanity throughout the ages concerns the mystery of death. My books are directed toward stimulating scientific interest toward solving that conundrum so that one day humanity will have the true answer and we no longer hide behind the base stupidity of ersatz religion. When we have mastered death we will become the gods and goddesses that we have invented in our vain attempt to escape our perceived horror of the Grim Reaper.

Appendix A

**THE INTERNATIONAL SOCIETY
FOR THE STUDY OF GHOSTS
AND APPARITIONS**

**Penthouse North
29 Washington Square West
New York, N.Y. 10011 USA**

THE INTL. SOCIETY FOR THE STUDY OF GHOSTS AND AND APPARITIONS

The history of the ISSGA dates back to the early 1980s when, on a visit to Chicago, the (eventual) founder of the society, Dr. Jeanne Keyes Youngson, met a ghost hunter who specialized in local spirit lore. Upon hearing of Youngson's fascination with the ghost world, the professional investigator invited her on a personally-conducted tour of Chicagoland's haunted areas which included a side trip to Al Capone's grave. The ghost hunter took a photograph of Youngson next to Al's tombstone and when the picture was developed, to everyone's surprise, a misty apparition seemed to be hovering to Youngson's right. No reason was ever found for the strange ghostlike specter that appeared on the film, nor did the photographer see anything odd when taking the photograph.

Youngson's fascination with ghosts increased when attending a conference at Corpus Christi College in Cambridge, England. Having arrived at the venue early, she was alone in the Old Court when at about 2 a.m. she was awakened by a sharp rapping on the wall directly behind her head. The following morning university porters told her about the college resident ghost, a former Master and Vice Chancellor, Dr. Henry Butts, who, in the 1700s, hung himself on the college grounds. The porters claimed that Butts only makes himself known to female visitors in the dead of night, although the top part of his body has been 'seen' by students in the early evening.

Youngson officially founded the ISSGA in 1985 and since 1990 has researched the spirit world in Malta, England, Ireland, Italy and Mexico, as well as many sites in the United States.

Club headquarters is located in a landmark building in historic Greenwich Village and 'the Prez' (as Youngson is known to members of both the Vampire Empire & the ISSGA) is well-known for her Village Ghost Walks that take place by pre-arrangement. Some of the places visited include: The El Charro Restaurant on Charles Street: Ghost: Romany Marie, the former San Remo & Kettle of Fish Bars: Ghost: Maxwell Bodenheim, the Firehouse on West Third: Ghost: a fireman who hung himself in the 1930s, etc. To top off the tour, Youngson points out the plaque on the front of 29 Wash. Sq. West, which indicates that Mrs. Eleanor Roosevelt once lived in the building. Mrs. R. has been seen wandering in the halls & most recently was sighted in the laundry by some workmen. Coincidentally, ISSGA Headquarters is in this building but alas, none of us has ever had the pleasure of coming face to face with the great lady.

OFFICERS OF THE ISSGA:

Dr. Jeanne Keyes Youngson,
PRESIDENT AND FOUNDER

Dr. Rosemary Ellen Guiley
Martin V. Riccardo
Dr. Stanley Krippner
VICE-PRESIDENTS

Nigel Watson (UK)
Thierry Breque (France)
EXECUTIVE DIRECTORS

Eric Held, Betsy Bell, Jim Martin,
Fred Francis, Lesley Bannatyne,
Stephen Grogan, Dr. Mark Benecke,
Fern Miller & Marjorie Keyes
SPECIAL ADVISORS

Ann Margret Hart
EXECUTIVE SECRETARY

RECOMMENDED READING:
Klein, Victor C. NEW ORLEANS GHOSTS
1&2. Metarie, LA. Lycanthrope Press.
Ludlam, Harry. TRUE GHOST STORIES.
Foulsom. London, 2000
Myers, Arthur. THE GHOSTLY REGISTER,
New York. Contemporary Books, Inc.

ABOUT THE FOUNDER

Dr. Jeanne Keyes Youngson was born in Syracuse, N.Y. and grew up in Sussex, N.J. She received her education at Franklin Junior College in Lugano, Switzerland, the Sorbonne and New York University. She has also taught extension courses in both Cambridge and Oxford Universities in England.

In 1965 she went to Romania on a guided tour and got the idea of starting a Dracula society which she founded upon her return to the USA. (Note: The original name of the society was THE COUNT DRACULA FAN CLUB. In the year 2000, the name was officially changed to THE VAMPIRE EMPIRE.)

In 1974 Youngson moved to England and established a counterpart club headquarters, first in London and later in Cambridge. She divided her time between the U.K. and the U.S.A. for several years, finally returning to America for good in 1982.

In 1985 she founded both the ISSGA and an American society dedicated to Bram Stoker, the first (and still only) Stoker club in the United States. Auxiliary memberships in both organizations are free to registered members of the Vampire Empire. Please write to club headquarters for further information

Appendix B

THE INTL. SOCIETY FOR THE STUDY OF GHOSTS AND APPARITIONS

Dear Victor:

I recently returned from New Orleans where my purpose was to photograph La Maison LaLaurie and see if I could pick up any vibes—(and to dine, of course).

I have both your ghost books...1 & 2...and find them of great help and interest.

As you can see by the enclosed flyer, I am very much into the genre myself. And what fun to live in a house haunted by Eleanor R.

I may be back in NOLA next March (or so) for a Tennessee Williams con. Perhaps we could get together for a little chat then. Or whenever...

Best regards,

Jeanne Keyes Youngson

29 Washington Square West, NYC, NY 10011

Appendix C

MARKETING AGREEMENT

This Marketing Agreement (hereinafter collectively the "Agreement") is entered into effective on the tenth day of May, 2001, between **ORDO TEMPLI VERITATIS** (hereinafter "OTV"), a non-profit corporation and the Reverend C. Klein, Ph.D. on the one hand, and **NEW ORLEANS GHOST TOURS, LLC** (hereinafter "Ghost Tours") a Louisiana limited liability company, appearing herein through Don R. Becker, Jr., member, on the other.

WHEREAS, Klein is the author of "New Orleans Ghosts" (hereinafter the "book") and OTV holds the copyright thereto.

WHEREAS, Ghost Tours operates and owns "The New Orleans Ghost Tour".

NOW, THEREFORE, the parties hereto agree as follows:

1. Klein and OTV hereby grant unto Ghost Tours, its successors and assigns, the right to reproduce and sell the book referred to above during the twelve month term of this agreement.

2. Klein and OTV further grant unto Ghost Tours the right to redesign the cover of said book by incorporating the brochure currently being used in connection with "The New Orleans Ghost Tour".

3. Ghost Tours initially agrees to purchase three thousand (3,000) copies of the book at a price of four dollars ($4.00) each or a total of twelve thousand dollars ($12,000.00), less three thousand four hundred dollars ($3,400.00) which is the cost to purchase and ship three thousand (3,000) copies from United Graphics of Matoon, Illinois, for a balance of eight thousand six hundred dollars ($8,600.00), to be paid in twelve equal monthly installments of seven hundred

sixteen dollars and sixty-seven cents ($716.67) each month commencing on June 15, 2001, and

monthly thereafter until paid. The principal balance shall bear no interest. Ghost Tours shall have

the right but not the obligation to purchase additional copies of the book for the same price and

under the same terms during the term of this Agreement.

4. Klein represents that OTV is the owner of the book and its copyright and that it has full

authority to enter into the Agreement and has not transferred or otherwise disposed of its

ownership thereof.

5. This Agreement and the rights of the parties hereunder will be governed by,
interpreted.

and enforced in accordance with the laws of the State of Louisiana.

6. In the event either party defaults under the terms of this Agreement, the prevailing
party

shall be due reasonable attorneys fees and costs in connection therewith.

7. If any provision of this Agreement is held to be illegal, invalid, or unenforceable under

the present or future laws effective during the term of this Agreement, such provision will be
fully

severable; and this contract will be construed and enforced as if such illegal, invalid, or

unenforceable provision had never comprised a part of this Agreement, and the remaining

provisions of this contract will remain in full force and effect and will not be affected by the

illegal, invalid, or unenforceable provision or by its severance from this Agreement.

IN WITNESS WHEREOF, the undersigned parties have executed this Agreement effective on the date first above written.

Witnesses:

NEW ORLEANS GHOST TOURS, LLC

By: Don K. Becker, Jr.

REVEREND C. KLEIN, Ph.D

ORDO TEMPLI VERITATIS

BY:REVEREND C. KLEIN,Ph.D

Appendix D

The 1850 House

in the

Lower Pontalba Building

A Historic Property of the Louisiana State Museum

Open Tuesday-Sunday
9:00 a.m. - 5:00 p.m.
Closed State Holidays

History and Architecture

Baroness Micaela Almonester de Pontalba constructed the two rows of town houses that flank Jackson Square on St. Ann and St. Peter Streets from 1849 to 1851 on land that she had inherited from her father, Don Andrés Almonester y Roxas. (Don Andrés, a wealthy Spaniard, had rebuilt the Cabildo, Presbytere and St. Louis Cathedral after the fire of 1788 destroyed the buildings previously on the sites, along with most of the old city.) Micaela engaged noted local architect James Gallier, Sr. to design the row houses, though she dismissed him before construction was begun, and she employed Samuel Stewart as the builder. She also hired another important New Orleans architect, Henry Howard, to work on the architectural drawings. Micaela's business relationships with Gallier, Stewart, and Howard were unsatisfactory to them and to her.

Micaela had been married some years before to Joseph Xavier Celestin de Pontalba, her cousin, and they lived in France. Although their union produced several children, the marriage was unhappy and turbulent and it ended in separation.

While living in France, the Baroness began to plan improvements on her property in New Orleans, the value of which was declining because of rival commercial development on Canal Street. She wanted to alter the Place d'Armes (parade ground), persuading the city authorities to rename it Jackson Square after General Andrew Jackson, the hero of the Battle of New Orleans, so that it would resemble the great public squares of Europe, such as the Palais Royal and the Place des Vosges in Paris. She proposed to build the two rows of town houses herself and she convinced municipal authorities to renovate the Square, Cabildo and Presbytere and church authorities to enlarge the Cathedral. Because of her difficulties with her architects and builder, the Baroness herself carefully and directly supervised much of the construction of her row houses. When the Pontalba Buildings were completed, each contained sixteen separate houses on the upper floors and self-contained shops on the ground floors. The "A & P" cartouches that decorate the cast-iron railings signify the Almonester and Pontalba families. Madame de Pontalba's buildings represent one of the first major American uses of industrially produced and nationally or internationally distributed building materials: New England granite, Baltimore pressed brick, English plate glass, English slates and roofing tiles, New York ornamental iron, New Jersey window glass, and Northern flagging.

The construction of the Pontalba row houses was intended to help stop the increasing deterioration of the old part of the city that had begun in the 1840s. Although the first residential tenants generally were from the middle and upper-middle classes, the neighborhood and row houses declined after the Civil War and, by the turn of the century, the Pontalba

2

Buildings had become tenements. William Ratcliffe Irby, a New Orleans philanthropist who was a pioneer in the preservation of historic landmarks in the French Quarter, bought the Lower Pontalba Building from the Pontalba heirs in 1921 for $68,000 and willed it to the Louisiana State Museum. In 1927, a year after Mr. Irby's death, the Museum came into possession of the building. The City of New Orleans ultimately acquired the Upper Pontalba Building on the opposite side of Jackson Square.

During the 1930s the Works Progress Administration, a federal job program, employed construction workers to do extensive restoration work on both Pontalba Buildings, and the town houses were subdivided into apartments. Restoration work on the Lower Pontalba Building continues to be an ongoing Museum project. In 1955 the Louisiana State Museum restored the interior of this building, #523 St. Ann Street, and the rooms of the second and third floors were furnished as examples of a fine town house in New Orleans in the 1850s.

Store

The first floors of the Pontalba Buildings were divided into individual stores that were rented to both wholesale and retail dealers. The residential quarters above the stores generally were rented separately. The glass store fronts, an English innovation of the 1840s, admitted light and displayed goods to their best advantage. The floors of the shops originally were cypress. There were no doors from the stores to the courtyards or the residential entrance passages. Among the shops found in the Pontalba Buildings in the 1850s were hardware, clothing, and dry goods stores. The first commercial tenant in this shop area was Adolphe Lanauze, a native of France who was a hardware merchant. Today, this shop houses the Museum gift shop.

The House, Its Tenants and Its Furnishings

Over the years, since the Louisiana State Museum opened the 1850 House as a period house museum, it has grown in sophistication and historical accuracy, thanks to many donations of furniture and decorative arts of the 1850s and also as a result of continuing research by the Museum curatorial staff on decorative arts, household technology, and domestic life in the United States and particularly in New Orleans in the mid-19th century. Since this house was constructed as a speculation property and most tenants did not remain in residence long, the furnishing plan is not based upon any person or family who lived here, but it does reflect mid-19th century prosperity, taste, and daily life in New Orleans.

The original tenants of the 1850 House were A.A. and Isaac Sovia. At this writing no further information is known about them

Domestic Technology

When Madame Pontalba first rented her town houses, she provided a gas line pipe that ran from the gas company's main gas line in the street to the inside surface of the front hall of each house, a water hydrant in each of the yards that was joined to the main pipes of the water works company in the street, a bell pull for each house entrance with a porcelain knob and bell, and water closets in each house. Tenants were responsible for any additional technological amenities.

Hallways

Access to the house was through this side corridor entrance. The ceiling has been lowered to conceal air conditioning and heating equipment. The walls and ceiling originally were painted with lime paint, the walls white and the ceilings light gray. The woodwork was painted with white lead oil paint. The same color scheme was used in the stair hall and the halls on the second and third floors, although along the stairs and in the upper halls, the lower baseboards were a gray-brown color. The stairs and risers were unpainted. The flagstone paving in the entrance hall and stair hall, although not original, is in keeping with the original architectural specifications.

Parlor

The woodwork in both the parlor and dining room originally was painted with white lead-in-oil paint, the lower baseboards with gray-brown lead-in-oil paint and the ceilings, ceiling cornices and medallions in both rooms with light gray lime paint. These rooms originally were wallpapered. They currently are painted with white lime paint, as were all the other rooms in the house. The tenant would have purchased and paid for the installation of the wallpaper and the gasoliers; also for the gas lines that ran from the first floor entrance to the parlor and dining room ceilings. The marble mantels and coal grates were included in the original architectural specifications, as were the interior window shutters in the parlor. The carpets and window hangings in both rooms are accurate period reproductions.

Families gathered around and entertained visitors in the parlor, which reflected a family's wealth, dignity and cultural development. Parlors of the mid-19th century were decorated to be instructive as well as attractive and they were filled with historical and

4

religious objects, figurines, musical instruments, furniture, flowers, games, decorative objects, and specimens from nature, such as seashells. Matching sets of parlor furniture became popular and affordable in the 1850s. A standard parlor set consisted of one or two sofas; a gentleman's chair with a high back and no arms; a lady's chair without arms that allowed for a woman's skirt and several side chairs with no arms. The majority of the furniture in the parlor of the 1850 House is in the Rococo Revival Style. This style is known for its bold curves and richly carved decorations inspired by the French Rococo period of the 18th century. The walls of the parlor are decorated with period oil on canvas landscapes and portraits. All accessories in the parlor date from the mid-19th century.

Dining Room

The dining room, like the mid-19th century parlor, was carefully decorated by the lady of the house to reflect the family's financial situation and social position. In this room the family gathered several times a day to eat meals and to converse about their daily activities. Servants prepared meals in the kitchen on the ground floor and carried food up the service wing stairs and through the dining room doors. A dinner table might be set with six or more entrées. The seventy-five piece *Vieux Paris* or "Old Paris" tableware set on the sideboard is an unusual survival of a complete set. *Vieux Paris* porcelain was imported into New Orleans by the barrel full from France. The porcelain on display compliments the mahogany and rosewood furniture, brass candelabra, and upholstered chairs of the period. Wall decorations include period alabaster wall plates and two oil on canvas portraits from Louisiana. The tablecloth and napkins date from the mid-19th century.

Bedrooms

The mantels of the fireplaces in all three bedrooms are made of wood painted as *faux marbre*, imitating the elegant marble mantels of the public rooms downstairs.

The master bedroom, where the lady of the house might have planned her daily household activities and pursued her hobbies such as painting, sketching and assorted needlework, contains a complete set of bedroom furniture, c. 1850-60, Rococo Revival Style, made in New Orleans by unknown cabinetmakers, but thought to be retailed by Prudent Mallard, a prominent local furniture dealer. This set of furniture was owned by Mrs. Magin uig of 624 Royal Street, whose portrait hangs above the mantel. The *Prie-Dieu*, or kneeler, and the oil on canvas *Sacred Heart of Jesus*, painted by an unknown mid-19th century New Orleans artist, reflect that New Orleans was largely a Roman Catholic city during this period.

5

All decorative arts, accessories, textiles and clothing used in this bedroom, as well as those displayed in the other two bedrooms, are of the period.

The gentleman's bedroom is decorated with furniture of the older and therefore the less popular styles of Gothic Revival and American Empire. It was common to use less fashionable furniture in less important rooms of a house. The dresser with mirror and full tester bed allegedly were made by slaves on a plantation in what is now the Carrollton section of the city. Wall decorations include a hand-colored lithograph of Jenny Lind, a famous Swedish vocalist who performed in New Orleans for several months in 1851 and who, while here, lived in one of the Upper Pontalba row houses; a small painting of Christopher Columbus and a painting of an American Indian scene.

Notice the two built-in closets on each side of the hall between the gentleman's bedroom and the master bedroom. These are original to the house and were unusual in the mid-19th century. The interior window shutters in the gentleman's bedroom and the nursery also are original to the house.

The nursery furniture reflects changing attitudes in the mid-19th century toward child rearing. Childhood came to be recognized as a formative period, easily influenced and directed by attentive adults. A well-stocked nursery included toys, music boxes, books and other amusements designed to keep the children well occupied within the confines of the room. Accompanied by their nurse, the children would make a brief evening appearance downstairs in the parlor to spend time with the rest of the family. Except for these evening visits and regular outdoor activities, young children of the mid-19th century spent most of their day in the security of the nursery.

Among the pieces of furniture in this room are a day bed, c. 1850; an American Empire table with marble top, c. 1835; a mid-19th century crib, a Gothic Revival wash stand, c. 1845-65 and a 19th century child's walker. The wall decorations include an alabaster wall plate and an oil on canvas painting of the Madonna and child. The numerous period toys in the room reflect the fact that mass production greatly increased the availability, number and variety of toys used by children of the mid-19th century.

Attic & Service Wing

The attic was equipped with fireplaces, so that it could be used for sleeping quarters for servants. It was also used for storage. The attic is not open to the public.

6

Proceed down the back stairs through the door near the master bedroom.

The back rooms of the row houses were originally used for a variety of different purposes depending on the size and needs of the family. Originally, each of the two upper floors contained two separate rooms with *faux marbre* mantels. The rooms on the upper floors of the service wing could have been used as a study for the gentleman of the house or as a bathing area. In the 1850 House, the top floor has been installed as a gentleman's study and the two rooms on the second floor have been installed as a bedroom and a bathing room. All furnishings and accessories date from the mid-19th century. Note that the top floor partition between the two original rooms has been removed and that the mantels in the rooms on the second floor have been removed and a doorway has been cut between the two rooms.

As you descend the service stairs, note the former location of the water closets on each floor. Today, these are modern restroom facilities and/or storage closets. The exterior walls of the service building and the courtyard walls originally were whitewashed for cleanliness. The arched opening in the courtyard was closed with a temporary brick fill. This arch was included in order that, if desired by the tenants, it could be opened if two related families rented these adjoining town houses.

Courtyard & Kitchen

The courtyard was a service area in which coal was stored for the cooking stove and fireplaces, laundry was dried and other household tasks were performed. It was never used as a recreation area. The flagstones in the courtyard are not original, but they are very similar to the original paving. The water hydrant that was connected to the city waterworks was located in the courtyard. City water came from the Mississippi River and had to be filtered to eliminate silt and sand. The privy vault, which was located beneath the water closets, regularly had to be cleaned of waste. This was done by a vault cleaner.

The kitchen and laundry open onto the courtyard. Both of these rooms had cypress floors. Note the cooking stove in the kitchen fireplace. It was manufactured in New York around 1850. Also notice the 19th century cooking utensils and crockery. The laundry is now an office and is not open to the public.

Exit the 1850 House through the door from the courtyard to the Museum Shop. This opening originally was a window.

--Revised **April, 2000**

Other Louisiana State Museum Buildings in the French Quarter:

The Presbytere on Jackson Square. Originally built in 1797 and intended to be the home for the priests of St. Louis Cathedral, the structure is now the home of *Mardi Gras: It's Carnival Time In Louisiana*. This fascinating, interactive exhibit explores the history, evolution, and celebration of Carnival throughout Louisiana through audio, video, and artifacts. From the amazing, handmade Mardi Gras Indian costumes, to "crown jewels," to fabulous finery worn by "royalty," to rural customs, this 16,000 square foot installation is certain to be fun for the entire family.

The Cabildo on Jackson Square. Site of the signing of the Louisiana Purchase Transfer, and the flagship building of the LSM, the Cabildo reopened in early 1994 following a five-year, multimillion dollar restoration. The Cabildo houses an exhibition about the history of Louisiana and New Orleans from exploration through the Civil War and Reconstruction, interpreting major events and historical themes from a multicultural perspective. **The Arsenal,** which is adjacent to the Cabildo, houses two long-term exhibitions: *Freshly Brewed: The Coffee Trade and the Port of New Orleans* and *Louisiana and the Mighty Mississippi River.* Admission to these exhibits is included with regular Cabildo admission.

The Old U.S. Mint on Esplanade Avenue across from the French Market. The oldest existing U.S. Mint building and the Civil War's only Confederate Mint, the large landmark now houses the State Museum's popular exhibitions on New Orleans Jazz and Newcomb Pottery. In addition, the facility also hosts traveling exhibitions. Ask any Museum cashier for the latest information.

Madame John's Legacy, 632 Dumaine St., is a rare example of early Creole residential architecture and houses one exhibit on the building's long history and another of folk art.

All State Museum properties are open
Tuesday through Sunday, 9:00 a.m. - 5:00 p.m. Closed State Holidays.
Discounted combination tickets are available.

For additional information, please call toll free at
(800) 568-6968
or write the Louisiana State Museum
P.O. Box 2448
New Orleans, LA 70176-2448

Website: http://lsm.crt.state.la.us

Appendix E

CORONER'S OFFICE

An Autopsy, held in the City of New Orleans, in the Parish of Orleans, on the 26th day of May in the year of our Lord, One Thousand Nine Hundred and _____

Before Me, C. W. Grossach, _____ Coroner for the said Parish of Orleans, on the view of the dead body of Mr. Johann Sciambra then and there lying dead. City Morgue

The Jurors, whose names are hereunto subscribed, having been duly sworn and charged diligently to inquire, on behalf of the State of Louisiana, how, when, and after what manner the said Mr. Johann Sciambra came to his death, and upon their oaths do say that after viewing an autopsy of said body declare the death was the result of penetrating gun shot wound of abdomen —

cause the following certificate of death to be given by the Coroner.

Name, _____ Sex, _____ Color _____
Native of _____ Aged _____ years, _____ months, _____ days,
a resident of this city since _____ by occupation _____
resident at No. _____ , died of
_____ on _____ 194_ , at _____ o'clock, _____

In Testimony Whereof, The said Coroner and Jurors of this inquest have hereunto subscribed their names the day and the year aforesaid.

State of California - Health and Human Services Agency Data Center   Department of Health Services

CERTIFICATION OF NO RECORD

This is to certify that an examination has been made of the Statewide Index in the Office of State Registrar of Vital Statistics covering the event shown and no reference to this event was found therein.

Name(s)

JOSEPH MUMFRE

Event	Period Search	
	From:	Through
Death	1905	2000

OFFICE OF
STATE REGISTRAR

Chief

Date   September 10, 2001

Acknowledgments

1. Keith Nicholson my faithful friend, computer genius and typist whose skills and perseverance have contributed to the completion of this book and many, many future successes and victories.

2. Juliette Couret Klein my mother who has provided invaluable aid in editing this work and supporting me through her love.

3. Jonathon Eric Mills my son who provides me with the hope of a future.

4. Don Becker who owns and operates *New Orleans Ghost Tours* for his honesty and encouragement.

5. Tulane University's Louisiana Collection for their help and support. Also, for preserving my papers for future seekers of the unknown. Libraries preserve civilization.

6. To all the women I have loved, who through sharing sex and love have helped me understand death.

7. Finally, to my father Victor Henry Klein who taught me about human potential through his example of discipline and, more importantly — Love.

Bibliography

Asbury, Herbert. The French Quarter. New York: Thunders Mouth Press, 1936.

Brock, Eric J. Images of America New Orleans Cemeteries. Charleston, SC: Arcadia Publishing, 1999.

Brown, Alan. Shadows and Cypress Southern Ghost Stories. Jackson, MS: University Press of Mississippi, 2000.

Cable, George W. Strange True Stories of Louisiana. Gretna, LA: Pelican Publishing Co., 1999.

Clark, Jerome. Unexplained. Detroit: Visible Ink, 1993.

Coleman, Christopher K. Dixie Spirits. Nashville, TN: Cumberland House, 2002.

deLaurence, L. W. The Greater Key of Solomon. Chicago: 1914.

deLavigne, Jeanne. Ghost Stories of Old New Orleans. New York: Rinehart & Co., 1946.

Dickinson, Joy. Haunted City: An Unauthorized Guide to the Magical, Magnificent New Orleans of Anne Rice. New York: Kensington Publishing Corp., 1998.

Edwards, Paul, Editor-in-Chief. The Encyclopedia of Philosophy. New York, London: Collier MacMillan Publishers, 1967.

Fox, Frank. Bizarre New Orleans. New Orleans: St. Expedite Press, 1997.

Gandolfo, Henri. Metairie Cemetery: An Historical Memoir. New Orleans: Stewart Enterprises, 1981.

Garvey, Joan B. And Widmer, Mary Lou. Beautiful Crescent A History of New Orleans. New Orleans: Garmer Press, Inc., 1984.

Gayarré's History of Louisiana, Volume III.

Guiley, Rosemary Ellen. The Encyclopedia of Ghosts and Spirits. New York: Checkmark Books, 2000.

Guiley, Rosemary Ellen. The Encyclopedia of Witches and Witchcraft (2nd ed.) New York: Checkmark Books, 1999.

Huber, Leonard V. New Orleans A Pictorial History. New York: Crown Publishers, Inc., 1971.

Klein, Victor C. New Orleans Ghosts, Metairie, LA: Lycanthrope Press, 1996.

Klein, Victor C. New Orleans Ghosts II, Metairie, LA: Lycanthrope Press, 2000.

Laughlin, Clarence John. Ghosts Along the Mississippi. New York: Bonanza Books, 1951.

Leavitt, Mel. A Short History of New Orleans. San Francisco: Lexikos, 1982.

Montz, Larry, & Daena Smoller. The Ghosts of New Orleans. Atglen, PA: Whitford Press, 2000.

Rose, Al. Storyville, New Orleans. Tuscaloosa, AL and London: The University of Alabama Press, 1974.

Reveaux, J. J. Haunted Bayou and Other Cajun Ghost Stores. Little Rock, AR, 1994.

Sadoul, Jacques. Alchemists and Gold. New York: GP Putnam's Sons, 1972.

Saxon, Lyle et al. Gumbo Va -Va. Gretna, LA, 1998.

Sillery, Barbara. The Haunting of Louisiana. Gretna, LA: Pelican publishing Company, 2001.

Smith, Kalila Katherina. Journey into Darkness: Ghosts and Vampires of New Orleans. New Orleans, LA: De Simonin Publications, 1998.

Spence, Lewis. An Encyclopedia of Occultism, New Hyde Park, New York: University Books, 1960.

Stall, Gaspar J. "Buddy". Louisiana COD (Cities of the Dead). Metairie, LA: Gaspar J Buddy Shall, 2000.

Stewart, Mollie. Ghosts Among Us. Salem: Curry Printing, 2001.

Taylor, Joe Gray. Louisiana A History. New York: WW Norton & Company, 1976.

Williams, Claudia. Haunted Spaces. New Orleans: Starling Publications, Ltd., 2004.

INDEX

To order additional copies of any of Victor C, Klein's works, please complete the order form below:

New Orleans Ghosts III $12.00
New Orleans Ghosts II $12.00
New Orleans Ghosts 12.00
Soul Shadows 12.00
Hermes and Christ 20.00
My Motto Is 6.00
A Poor Store 100.00
Academic Papers XI Vols. 2,000.00

Order Form

Name_____

Street Address_____

City_____State_____

Zip Code_____Daytime phone_____

e-mail address_____

TITLE	Quantity	PRICE	TOTAL

TOTAL . . . . _____

Price includes postage and handling. **Same Day Shipping.**

Money Orders <u>only</u> payable to:
Ordo Templi Veritatis
Post Office Box 9028

This is Victor C. Klein's third and last book in the *New Orleans Ghosts* series. The author was born and reared in New Orleans. He loves the Crescent City and considers it as a woman who has never betrayed him; nor has he betrayed her.

All of the *New Orleans Ghosts* books are anthropologically significant works in that they contain addresses, indexes, footnotes, bibliographies, photographs and ephemera. They are created to entertain, inform *and* challenge. The author hopes that the reader enjoys his efforts. Please note that the photograph above is the author's dog, Wolfen, and not, I repeat *not* the author.